The Diary of an

EMOTIONALLY CONSTIPATED MAN

By

Dr. William "Flip" Clay

Disclaimer

Some names and identifying details have been changed to protect the privacy of individuals.

This book is designed to provide information and motivation to our readers. It is sold with the understanding that the publisher is not engaged to render any type of psychological, or any other kind of professional advice.

The content of the book is the sole expression and opinion of its author. No warranties or guarantees are expressed or implied by the author. This book is not intended as a substitute for the medical advice of physicians. The reader should regularly consult a physician in matters relating to his/her health and particularly with respect to any symptoms that may require diagnosis or medical attention. You are responsible for your own choices, actions, and results.

Acknowledgements

This book is dedicated to the memory of my parents, William and Annie Mae Clay, who raised me to serve others and become a person of influence with the power to change lives. Their legacy of love and compassion will continue to manifest itself.

Table of Contents

Preface 1

Introduction 6

Chapter 1: Emotional Psychological Incarceration 8

Chapter 2: You Have to Reveal to Heal 19

Chapter 3: The Day I Divorced Religion 28

Chapter 4: Man Down: Father Gone 40

Chapter 5: Emotional Detoxification 51

Chapter 6: Love, Lies, and Emotions 63

Chapter 7: The Inner Me Is the Enemy 73

Chapter 8: Intergenerational Emotional Incarceration 82

Chapter 9: The Excavation of Emotions 93

Chapter 10: Traffic-Light Healing 103

Chapter 11: The Laxative 106

Conclusion 115

References 117

About the Author 119

Preface

I can recall my first job after completing my master's degree. I had completed college in December and was hired the following January to work in a predominately white school district in Northern Virginia as an elementary school counselor.

As an elementary school counselor, I felt like I could make a difference because of what I went through as a child. I was an itinerate counselor assisting the school-based counselors with their duties. I was assigned to four schools. I loved the idea of going to four different schools and meeting the various parents, students, and teachers. It seemed to me that every teacher wanted me to speak with all the boys, especially the black boys. I felt like a star. My success came from the fact that I was energetic, crazy, creative, down to earth, funny, and engaging; and I spoke to kids on their level.

I've always had a passion for helping children, especially black boys. Teachers would always ask, "What did you say to them? They have changed their behavior!" I didn't do anything special; I was just myself. My first year was a great learning experience. I learned to deal with those teachers, parents, and others who didn't like me because of the color of my skin, while taking pleasure in interacting with those who loved me because I loved children.

I can recall my first real eye-opener as a counselor. A teacher – I'll call her Ms. K – stated, "Mr. Clay, I really need to speak with you about one of my students."

I said, "Okay, what's wrong?"

"Well, we were drawing snowman pictures, and one of my students asked for his picture back because he wanted to put snowflakes on it."

I was confused. "What's wrong with snowflakes?" I asked.

"Well, he put the snowflakes on the chest of the snowman and called them boobies."

She then told me, "I'm also concerned because he has a girlfriend in the classroom."

I stood there thinking, *He's five. What does he know about boobies and girlfriends?* I had to figure out how I was going to talk to this child about snowflake boobies on a snowman. I always kept magazines around because pictures were a good conversation point for kids. As I went through my magazines, I found the *Sports Illustrated* swimsuit edition. I brought the boy in and asked him to look through the magazine and tell me which pictures he liked. I watched him turn the pages, and when he saw those women in the swimsuits, his eyes widened.

I asked, "Why do you like those pictures so much?"

He said, "Because my mommy has snowflakes. We take showers, and we watch movies together." He continued, "And Ms. K's snowflakes are larger than Ms. W's snowflakes."

"How do you know?" I asked.

He replied, "Because me and my two friends call them to the table; and when they come to the table, we look at them when they bend over to help us."

"Okay," I answered slowly. I moved on to the next question. "So I heard you have a girlfriend?"

"Yes, I have two girlfriends. One girl is real quiet, but the other one talks back to her mom a lot. The quiet one is in my class."

"How do you know the other girl talks back to her mom?"

"I go over to her house and stay overnight and play in the backyard. We kiss in the backyard but don't tell my parents."

I then asked, "What kind of movies do you watch with your mommy?" He said, "Snowflake movies."

I said, "okay" and told him I was going to send him back to class. As we walked back to class, I was in shock. I spoke with Ms. K, and she was shocked as well. She told me that it explained why they kept calling Ms. W (the teacher's assistant) and her to their table.

Next, I had to talk to the parents. How was I going to tell a stay-at-home mother that her son told me they watched snowflake movies and took showers together? Well, I explained the story to the mother and she told me that, yes, they did take showers together. And when he was younger, they would watch movies as a family, but she never thought he was really paying attention because he was two years old at the time. I explained that kids are very curious and asked her to please be careful what she did in front of her children.

After that incident, I knew school counseling was my calling. During my tenure in that Virginia school system, I met some beautiful people. I'll never forget Brenda Herman, a white school counselor who was the spitting image of me. She loved the children, and everything she did exemplified enthusiasm, energy, love, and passion. I enjoyed going to her school, and it gave me the opportunity to see firsthand a young, white female working with black boys.

I'll also always remember Linda Falden, a black school counselor who adopted me as a son. She would always give me words of encouragement. During my tenure in Northern Virginia, there were people who thought I was too "urban." I was teaching guidance lessons using rap, rhymes, and rhythms. I would say things to children in their language, and several people didn't approve of my techniques. I never let that stop me from helping the children. I wanted kids to learn about proper behavior in an engaging manner.

As time progressed, I started building a better rapport with all the children. Several of the children would call me "daddy." I never had a problem with it because I understood why they did it; growing up, my father didn't live in my house, just like many of theirs. A lot of people thought it wasn't right though, so I had to start telling the kids to stop. I can recall the look on the black kids' faces when I told them not to call me daddy; it was heartbreaking. The white kids very seldom said it; but every now and then, it did occur.

I can recall one particular Friday when I was on bus duty. On bus duty days, the kids would always run up and give me hugs. On this particular day, there was a white girl and a black girl waiting to say goodbye.

The white girl said, "Bye, Daddy."

The black girl told her, "He is not your father!"

The white girl replied, "In God's eyes, he is."

When she said that, time froze for me. I went to my office and tried to fight the tears. Here was a child who didn't see color, only the godly love I had for children. After a short tenure in that school district, I was told they weren't going to offer me another contract. Even my principal was surprised.

He told me, "You're a real good counselor, Mr. Clay. I hate to lose you."

I was upset that the school district didn't offer me another contract, but sometimes Yahweh allows us to "go through to get to." As a result, I was hired by a school district that was predominately black. I started working at my first school. During my interview, I was warned that the principal was crazy and the kids were off the hook. I remember going into the class to introduce myself. I carried my pet brick around during my introduction. On my pet brick was written my name and the words, "He is crazy!"

I gained the respect of the older kids. During my tenure, I decided to take counseling black boys to another level. I started forming data-driven successful empowerment programs throughout my district. The programs were lifechanging. I was shocked that people were so accepting compared to my last school district. The feedback from the parents was extraordinary. Furthermore, I've spent the last 17 years changing the lives of children, youth, parents, and more.

As a result of my success, I started my own educational consulting practice. I began presenting at local conferences, schools, churches, and community agencies. I can recall speaking at my first national conference in Atlanta, Georgia. My mentor, Erik Cork, introduced me at the National Association of Black School Educators' national conference. There were over 150 people in the room, and I was nervous; people from all over the country were there to hear me. I was the bomb!

As time progressed, my empowerment program went to yet another level. I could see the lives of black boys changing daily. Now, several years later, I know it's time to share my journey with parents, teachers, counselors, community service workers, and other people working with children or youth in any capacity.

Introduction

One of the major issues facing young people, especially males of color, is their perception about expressing their emotions and mental health. Significant changes are needed in how males view mental health. Systematic reforms must be undertaken to deal with the mental health crisis in America. In addition, these reforms must include the public school system.

These reforms are needed because mental health is an equal-opportunity virus. It affects people from all walks of life, be they rich or poor, young or old, black or white. Unfortunately, some groups are more vulnerable to a mental health crisis than others. Mental health usually impacts those living in poverty and those who face discrimination. Research shows that, of the 45.7 million black people living in the United States, 16% had a diagnosable mental illness in the past year – that's over 6.8 million people walking around with diagnosable yet likely untreated mental illnesses. African-Americans of all ages are also more likely to be victims of serious violent crime than their white counterparts, making them more likely to meet the diagnostic criteria for post-traumatic stress disorder (9).

There are several variables that hinder black men and many low-income people back from seeking mental health treatment. The cost is a major variable. Furthermore, males often don't know where to turn when they don't see mental health signs hanging in their neighborhoods or schools. Breaking the silence and reducing stigmas around seeking care is only the first step in breaking down generational curses. With so few services offered to low-income residents, and even fewer offered by black-owned, community-based institutions, those in need of care often lack access to the affordable services that would make the greatest impact on their health.

While stigma around mental illness is widespread, there is a particularly insidious silence by males of all ages, races, and religion. The purpose of writing this book is to share my story with the world with the hopes that one person will feel comfortable doing the same and help them have the courage to release. Get ready to take an emotional journey through the lives of several people of all ages, races, and cultures who represent the human race.

CHAPTER 1

Emotional Psychological Incarceration

"Your emotions are the slaves to your thoughts, and you are the slave to your emotions."

– Elizabeth Gilbert

In order to understand the present, you must understand the past. I remember growing up as a little boy. I was confused about my life. Why did I have to go through so much? Why did I watch my mother die? Why did I watch my father mistreat her? Why did she suffer for so many years? Why did she step on a piece of tar, which then caused cancer?

It was always on my mind: Why me? Those questions weren't answered until I left home and attended Charleston Job Corps. Sometimes you must leave your current environment to truly see your future.

I recall being interviewed by this newspaper. One of the main questions was why I left home for Job Corps and what did I want to become when I left it? I recall saying to the reporter, "I want to become a probation officer or counselor." My goal in life was to help children, youth, and everyone else overcome challenges.

Now, after 17 years of walking in my purpose, I want to share with you real stories of obstacles, challenges, and the impact counselors make every day. The very first question I want to ask the reader is this: Do you think that, when you are exposed to trauma, you are crazy if you respond recklessly? I would assume no! What does the mental health field say about the impact of trauma? How are counselors impacted?

I want to introduce you to Candy. She was diagnosed with post-traumatic stress disorder (PTSD), anxiety, and major depression. I met Candy several years ago back when she didn't trust   people, especially men. I remember my first encounter with her. It was crazy! I could see the look in her eyes. I was black.

"You're my counselor?"

"Yes."

I recall sharing my life story with her. She was shocked. I was very transparent, but it took months to build her trust. Candy shared with me how her mother's boyfriend, Paul, molested her and how she felt. She felt dirty inside. She felt like throwing up! You could see the pain. Her eyes spoke to my spirit.

I was only the second person she felt comfortable going into detail about her story. She didn't trust anyone, but I finally was able to break through. I was honored. I was black, and it's hard for victims of molestation to trust. I knew the journey would be long. My first year with her was rough.

Candy hated herself. She would cut herself. She didn't like taking showers. The water reminded her of his hands. But I never gave up on her; I was determined. My second year was better. I became the shining light. I became her ear to heaven. Her mother even stated that I was helping her baby girl.

Candy was a better person. She wasn't cutting herself as often as before. She loved drawing pictures of her pain and happiness. The pictures served as her guide. They were powerful. Candy started making progress. She didn't feel dirty anymore. Her drawings became better. She was talking more!

I was so proud Candy wasn't afraid anymore. My time spent with her could never be replaced. Our conversations, tears, and laughter will always be memorable. I remember teaching her about how thoughts create reality. I shared how we must get rid of "Stinking Thinking" because it smells like poop.

"How does it smell, Candy?"

She would laugh.

I will never forget the day she wrote this letter to her abuser.

Dear Paul:

I have a big question that I ask myself 'til this day, why? Why did you make my life miserable? I never did anything to you, yet you still did what you "needed" to do.

How does it feel to open a book? I bet it felt great for you! You opened me up as if I were a book, looking at me as if you were scanning your eyes over words through each page. Each page flipped, the more I felt worse, but the worse part was when I had to pretend to "like" it because I knew that you would hurt me as if you were tearing a book apart. I'm a worn-out book that has gone through things, but I know for a fact you can't tear me apart from a girl you'll never bring down.

After reading this letter, I was shocked. She wasn't afraid anymore. My work was done, but her journey will continue. We all play a part in the journey of a wounded soul. Thank you, Candy!

An expected or culturally approved response to a common stressor, loss, or trauma (such as the death of a loved one) is not a mental disorder. Socially deviant behavior (e.g., political, religious, or sexual) and conflicts that are primarily between the individual and society are not mental disorders unless the deviance or conflict results from a dysfunction in the individual, as described above. There, is a behavioral or mental pattern that may cause suffering or a poor ability to cope. In other words, what is wrong with them?

All psychiatric diagnoses are categorized by the *Diagnostic and*

Statistical Manual of Mental Disorders, 5th. Edition. Better known as the DSM-5, the manual is published by the American Psychiatric Association and covers all mental health disorders for both children and adults. It also lists known causes of these disorders; statistics in terms of gender, age at onset, and prognosis; as well as some research concerning the optimal treatment approaches. A sample of disorders includes anxiety disorders, alcohol/substance disorder, depression, PTSD, adult attention deficit (ADD)/hyperactivity disorder, schizophrenia, and obsessive-compulsive disorder (1). Mental health professionals use this manual when working with patients in order to better understand their illness and potential treatment.

The DSM *Manual* is as important as the Bible to the preacher, the Quran to the imam, and the Torah to the rabbi. As time progressed, the term "mental health" became more popular. However, clinical psychology and social work developed as professions alongside psychiatry.

In the United States, a "mental hygiene" movement, originally defined in the 19th century, gained momentum and aimed to "prevent the disease of insanity" through public health methods and clinics. Theories of eugenics led to compulsory sterilization movements in many countries around the world for several decades, often encompassing patients in public mental institutions.

World War I saw a massive increase of conditions that came to be termed "shell shock." Its impact on men's mental health, especially black men's, is no secret. One of the challenges that the institution and black community as a whole often grapple with is how to provide support for black men who are dealing with addiction, depression, and other mental illness.

The question often posed in conversation among mental health professionals is why men, especially African-American men, shy away from psychotherapy as a potential solution to challenges such as depression, anxiety, PTSD, marriage problems, and parenting issues? There are several variables that cause black men not to seek therapy. They are cost, embarrassment, trust, cultural understanding, treatment, pride, weakness, money, and discrimination. Furthermore, despite being disproportionately affected by mental health conditions, black men in America have to deal with a lack of healthcare resources, a higher exposure to factors that can lead to developing a mental health condition, and a lack of education about mental health. These all serve as barriers to getting proper help.

As a counselor, it is awkward that so many men, especially African-American men, are reluctant to make use of psychology's solutions to emotional hurdles. According to the U.S. Department of Health and Human Services of Minority Health, black people are 10% more likely to report having serious psychological distress than white people (2). There's a stigma when it comes to black boys and men talking about their mental health. Men are often taught to suppress any expression of sadness during childhood. As a result, depression becomes very common among men; though very few are willing to admit it.

As a result, depression sometimes manifests through the ego, which hinders males from showing weakness, sadness, or vulnerability. Furthermore, men hide it and become angry, irritable, self-centered, ego-driven, workaholics, demanding, and alcoholics. After 17 years of counseling males successfully in the school, church, and community, and reminiscing on my life growing up, I became sick and tired of seeing males diagnosed and misdiagnosed, or the issue never being addressed.

Upon further research, I came upon world-renowned psychologist and Harvard University professor, Jerome Kagan. He claimed that attention deficit hyperactive disorder (ADHD) is an "invention" and doesn't actually exist.

I was shocked. I didn't know what to think. I knew for a fact that I had seen young people, especially students, with weird hyperactive behavior. Certainly, his view has gained much criticism from psychologists and other medical professionals. But Kagan, who was named the 22nd most eminent psychologist of the 20th century, has fiercely defended his viewpoint and insisted that there needs to be a shift in how mental health professionals issue medication.

He criticized the trend for diagnosing children who misbehave or underperform at school as having ADHD, claiming that doctors are too eager to write prescriptions before investigating the circumstances.

This, Kagan said, is "immoral and corruptive," leading to overdiagnoses and misdiagnoses in many cases. Kagan has defended his position, insisting that his views are far from an attack of those who suffer from mental health issues. Insisting that administering mind-altering drugs, especially to children, is a serious situation, he claimed there should be a deeper investigation into each patient's individual circumstances before a diagnosis is made.

Kagan said: "There are people who, either for prenatal or inherited reasons, have serious vulnerabilities in their central nervous system that predispose them to schizophrenia, bipolar disease, social anxiety or obsessive-compulsive disorders. We should distinguish these people..." He recommended that, rather than just looking at symptoms, diagnoses of mental health disorders should be made on a case-by-case basis – and that the entire system of how mental health issues are made needs to be reassessed to ensure the health and safety of the patient. Advocating medicine is not required in some cases.

I've seen my share of cases where medication is required. I've seen cases where medication worked. However, if males are misdiagnosed, what is wrong? The solution to the issue is *emotional* **psychological incarceration (EPI).** What is EPI? It is a nondiagnostic mental disorder triggered by trauma. It's usually triggered by divorce, ego, pride, embarrassment, shame, and guilt. There are other variables that may trigger a male to suffer from EPI. A nondiagnostic mental disorder means that the condition will not be listed in the DSM-5. Basically, in laymen's terms, this disorder is not recognized by any medical authority.

In my role as a consultant, I've been blessed to converse with parents, teachers, preachers, principals, and community members about males. In my role as a professional school counselor, I've seen firsthand the plight of males. A majority of teachers, educators, and parents have similar concerns. They state that some males are angry, frustrated, unfocused, irritable, can't sit still, have low self-esteem, and are lazy. In my role as a professional school counselor, I've observed the following emotions and reactions: blame, guilt, anger, anxiety, depression, aggression, avoidance, confusion, agitation, withdrawal, a tendency to be easily provoked, laziness, and pain.

I can recall numerous meetings with teachers that involved some male student who wouldn't sit still, couldn't focus, daydreamed, and/or seemed angry about something. I would think he has ADD/ADHD. Sometimes though, I doubted this because, deep down inside, I knew that was not the problem.

There are three phases of EPI that people, especially males, exemplify. The first is emotional constipation. This occurs from birth to age 14 (3). During this phase in emotional development, males exhibit behaviors that are contrary to society norms. They are as follows: can't sit still; too talkative; always moving around; predisposed to be angry, frustrated, unfocused, self-centered, unemotional, outspoken, rebellious, or attention-seeking; etc.

The second phase is emotional incarceration. This occurs between the ages of 14 to adulthood (3). Unfortunately, during this time period, males develop negative attitudes toward school, teachers, parents, life and society. They skip class, walk the halls, use profanity, mistreat girls, manipulate their parents, disrespect authority, use drugs, join gangs, and become less concerned about life and education. The only reason they come to school is to invalidate their insecurity.

In adulthood, they exemplify aggression, depression, identity crisis, and violence. They cry when alone at night. They seek love and acceptance from various means. They go into adulthood with the divide-and-conquer mindset. They seek relationships where they are in control. They lack trust. They search for validation. Some become sexual monsters. They carry the following additional traits into adulthood: They tend to feel ashamed, dehumanized, disrespected, embarrassed, humiliated, inferior, insulted, invalidated, labeled, mocked, offended, resentful, and ridiculed.

The third phase is physical incarceration. This is triggered by phase one and two. Though there are nearly 1.5 million black males in state or federal prison, their absence from public life is not accounted for in the figures that politicians and policymakers use to make decisions. I'm sure that 80% are emotionally constipated and incarcerated. Furthermore, they never discuss their issues. They are forced to face those issues when they are stuck behind bars.

For example, I recall five years ago when I was sitting in my office. The secretary called me to her desk.

"Dr. Clay, you have a new student. You should look through his file. He receives numerous services for his emotional disorders."

Dre was 14 years of age, but his life experience was that of a 20-year-old. His record included several assaults, four foster home placements, being kicked out of several schools, being abused as a child, being abused in foster homes, and being locked up three different times. He was court-ordered to attend my school until he could be placed in the right education setting. He was six feet tall and 180 pounds.

I introduced myself to him the first day. We sat in my office and talked for 45 minutes. I introduced him to Tupac. He was fascinated with his story. I became emotionally transparent with him about my life. He started asking questions. He was focused and listening. I invited him to my male empowerment program. He never responded to the invitation. His first two weeks were interesting. We didn't see any of the expected behaviors.

The following week was a different story. He stopped going to class. He was using profanity up and down the hallway. He became very disrespectful to female teachers. The students knew him. He was a street kid with street credibility. He didn't take anything from anybody. He was the man in school.

He started spending more time in my office. His behavior improved. He would have good days and bad days. He was trying. I remember him telling me how cool I was and how he trusted me. Several weeks passed, and thigs were okay. This was improvement compared to his other school. He did something and was suspended for three days. The suspension should have been longer, but we agreed to reduce the suspension if he joined the group. He agreed to attend the group upon return. Finally, he came to the group.

My group was powerful. My boys released, cried, laughed, and supported each other once a week. We were a family. We trusted each other like peanut butter and jelly. He was shocked to see young boys his age crying and sharing their stories. I recall one student in particular who told the group he wanted to kill his father. He wanted to kill him because his father had disowned him since birth. He saw another male student crying because of his father. He heard the boys talk about everything. He never spoke, but he was watching everything.

I saw him the next day.

"What's up, Dr. Clay?"

"I'm good, and you?"

"I'm good."

"How did you like the group?"

I didn't get a response.

I saw him again. "How did you like the group?"

I still didn't get a response.

Finally, it was time for our next group meeting. He was the first one in the room. He beat me there. I spoke and kept it moving. It was time for sharing. He raised his hand to speak. The boys were shocked. I was shocked too.

He said, "I was three years old, and my parents were on drugs. I recall standing at the top of the steps. My mother kicked me, and I rolled down the steps. I was taken from her and never saw her again until eight years later. I've been locked up, abused, and placed in several different foster homes. I'm angry and I'm trying to be tough, but it hurts."

He started to cry. He was fighting the tears. He came in my office the next day.

He said, "Thank you!" He said, "Dr. Clay, I don't like my psychiatrist. He is white, and I'm not crazy. He doesn't understand like you do! You know, Dr. Clay, this was the second time I've shared my story. It felt good."

I said, "No problem. This is what we do."

Several weeks passed, and he was doing okay. All of a sudden, the stuff hit the fan. One of the boys in group violated our confidential contract. He shared with someone Dre's story. This was his third violation. I returned to my office, and Dre was waiting.

"I'm going to f*** him up," he said. "He shared my story. He's been ducking me all day."

The president and two other people were looking for him. "Dr. Clay, you need to handle this as soon as possible."

The next day the president, myself, and the principal called a meeting. The young man entered my office. He was shaking and scared. He knew Dre was going to handle his business. We came to an agreement. Dre accepted his apology. He was removed from the group.

Dre continued in our school. He was starting to have problems with his foster mother. Dre tried to break into her home, and she called the police. A week later, she withdrew him from school. The mother stated he ran away from home. She reported him to social services and relinquished her rights.

Dre gained the power to release his constipation! Are you ready to release?

What did you learn from Dre/Candy?

_____

_____

_____

_____

How did Dre feel about his life?

_____

_____

_____

_____

Why did Dre love the group?

_____

_____

_____

_____

Why did Candy write the letter?

_____
_____
_____
_____

What advice do you have for Dre/Candy?

_____
_____
_____
_____

What did you learn from this chapter?

_____
_____
_____
_____

How did this chapter relate to you?

_____
_____
_____
_____

What was your greatest takeaway?

_____
_____
_____
_____

CHAPTER 2

You Have to Reveal to Heal

"One thing you can't hide is when you're crippled inside."

– John Lennon

I recall growing up with my family. It was my father, mother, sister and I. My sister was older than me. Our family was typical. My father was the breadwinner in the family. My sister was daddy's girl, and I was mama's boy. Our house was huge; it consisted of four bedrooms, two bathrooms, and a full basement. My room was close to the kitchen, and my playroom was downstairs. I was the happiest little boy in the world. I loved going to school, church, and spending time with my friends.

My best friend was Michael. He lived next door. He lived with his mother. He never really talked about his father. I never asked him questions about his father. I could tell he wished his father was in his life. I don't recall ever seeing or meeting his father. I thought this was strange. My sister and I got along pretty well. We would have disagreements but nothing we couldn't solve.

My parents would have their disagreements. My father was very moody. I never understood his behavior. He was angry, mad, and always on a mission. He loved the belt; he would tear me up for the least little thing. My mother would tell him to stop beating me so hard. He would always say I deserved it. I didn't earn those beatdowns. He was off the hook.

My parents started to argue more, and I was confused. We would go out in public, and everything was calm. I can recall hearing them argue day after day. My father was running the streets. He would come home drunk. He would call my mother every name in the book. He would smack, punch, and shake her. He would leave bruises on my mother. He would give her black eyes. He did everything possible to make her feel ashamed.

I was scared to say anything to him. I was only five years old and didn't know what to do. I finally told both of my grandmothers. My mother's mother was shocked because my mother never told her. My father's mother wasn't shocked. She loved her son but knew he was angry, crazy, and quick-tempered.

The abuse continued day after day, night after night. It was really getting to the point where I couldn't sleep at night. My mother would holler as he struck her and tell him to stop. I would run in my room and put my head under the pillow. Eventually, he would stop. I was really confused because he would beat my mother. He would tell her he was sorry. My parents would be intimate right after abusing her. I didn't know what to think.

I finally said to my mother, "Why does he hit you? Why don't you fight back?" My mother never answered my questions.

I didn't understand how you could love someone and abuse them at the same time. My mother continued to put up with his behavior. It was really bad on the weekends. It was so bad I didn't want to come home from school. I didn't want to see my father. I wanted to be with my grandmother. The only issue was that she lived 20 minutes away, and I would get in trouble if I called her too much.

We didn't have cellphones. We didn't have email. There was no Uber.

The abuse was so bad my mother would miss work and walk around clueless. She stopped being my mother. She stopped giving me kisses. She stopped living. She stopped loving. I was eight years of age.

The physical abuse was strong, but the verbal abuse was five times stronger. In those days, children stayed in their place and didn't question their parents. You definitely better not go to school or church talking about your parents fighting. I recall this one night in particular. I couldn't take it anymore. I ran out of the room. My father was hitting my mother.

She was yelling and trying to fight back. The more she fought, the harder he struck her. His back was turned to me. I remember picking up the lamp and striking him across his back. I ran into the room. My mother was shocked. My father was shocked. He stopped beating my mother, and I went to bed. I was scared to come out of my room the next day. Eventually, I came out of the room. I was shaking like shake and bake. I finally saw my father. He said to come in the room.

I remember looking at my mother. She wouldn't dare say anything after what he did the previous night. My father tore me up. He really put a nice whipping on me this particular time. He was crazy. He would talk while giving me a beating. His eyes were frightening.

My mother started having health issues. The abuse was taking a toll on her. You could see it was becoming unbearable. I remember how my mother became very secretive. She wouldn't say much. One day, all of a sudden, she started talking about leaving. She wanted to know who would my sister and I live with if they separated. I knew where I was going, and my sister felt the same way. My sister never really said anything or expressed her feelings to me.

Eventually, my mother decided that enough was enough. We had the support of our family, friends, and the church. My mother took notice of the impact on my sister and I. It was finally over. My mother was leaving my father. The abuse would stop. The fighting would stop. The pain would stop. This was the best news I ever heard in the world.

It was time to celebrate. This was life-changing. It was a new start. We would move to our own place. My father wouldn't be around anymore.

We finally moved to Round Top Avenue Apartments. Our apartment's sliding glass window was facing a cemetery; it scared me all the time. I would wake up at night looking for ghosts. Eventually, my mother started dating again. She met this man in the military. I remember he wore several stripes and things on his uniform.

He would come over to the apartment. I knew he was trying to do what my father and mother used to do in the bedroom. I was determined this was not going to occur. I went out of my way to make his visits miserable because I didn't like him. I would do things to make my mom stop giving him attention when he was getting too close. They eventually broke up.

I was happy, and life was going well. My mother was working a job. We didn't have much, but we had peace of mind. We were receiving welfare benefits. Our new apartment had three bedrooms and one bath. The only downside was the roaches. They were all over the place. We sprayed and tried everything possible to keep them away. I would go to sleep with roaches in my bed, on the wall, and all over the place. I recall getting up one night. I went to the fridge. I drank some Pepsi. I felt something in my mouth. I spit it out. It was a roach.

We didn't have a lot. My mother was doing her best. I didn't complain. I was thankful for peace of mind.

My celebration was short-lived. My mother was having health issues. She kept going to the doctor. She really didn't say much. Eventually, she broke down and told me what the doctor had discovered. My mother was diagnosed with Kaposi's Sarcoma. I remember seeing this dark mark on my mother's foot. It was Cancer. My mother continued to work. She would have good days and bad days. Finally, my mother decided to move to be closer to her family.

The doctor gave my mother three to five years to live. I was around 10 years of age. My sister moved with my father, and I stayed with my mother. We moved to the Dupont Garden apartments. Our apartment was on the second floor. My mother was still walking at this point.

We had some crazy neighbors. My mother would always give them whatever they requested. I would get mad. "Mom, what is wrong with you? They work every day. Why don't they have their own basic needs?" It went from food and money, to rides to different places. My mother would never say no! They were something else. I would get mad every time I saw them. They took advantage of my mother, and they knew she had a heart of gold.

My mother's cancer became more severe. I remember playing outside. It was getting late. The sun was going down. My mother came to the top of the steps. I was looking up. She said, "It's time for you to come into the house."

I said, "B****, I'm not coming in the house."

I don't know what overcame me to disrespect my mother. I felt so bad I didn't want to go into the house. I remember walking into the house with my head down. I told my mother I was sorry. She was hurt, but she accepted my apology. I remember sitting at the kitchen table.

My mother said, "I want to share something with you." She said, "I'm teaching you how to do things because, eventually, you going to take care of me. Furthermore, promise me two things: Never treat a women like your father treated me, and make something of yourself."

I thought about my father. As time passed, my mother was placed in the hospital. I was staying with my grandmother. The cancer was spreading up her leg and into her bloodstream.

The doctor told my mother, "If we don't amputate the leg, you won't live long."

My mother said, "No!"

She was adamant. My mother returned back to the apartment. She was in a wheelchair. We wouldn't be here long. Our apartment was upstairs. The cancer was spreading fast. My days were long. I went to school during the day. I came home and waited on my mother after school. This went on seven days a week for three years. My mother was taking about 20 pills a day. She couldn't talk anymore. She would moan when she was thirsty and hungry. I would feed her and do everything she taught me. I barely slept. I was up all through the night.

I recall falling asleep. My mother started moaning. I woke up. She needed to use the bathroom. I picked her up. When we got to the bathroom, I dropped her against the wall. I was tired. I got myself together. I cried once I returned to my room. I woke up the next day and went to school.

My life was falling apart. I was losing my mother, my heart, my love, and all hope. The days and nights were longer and longer. We continued to wait for another apartment. We needed something that was handicapped accessible. I was in middle school and trying to stay focused on my grades. My grades were slipping, and no one knew the severity of my mother's sickness.

I finally broke down and shared it with my school counselor. She would listen and give me the outlet I needed. Every little bit helped because we didn't have money to see a counselor.

If I recall correctly, it was Friday. I came home, waited on my mother and went to sleep. All of sudden, I heard this loud banging on the door. I woke up the house was full of smoke. The apartment under us had caught on fire. The smoke came through the vents and filled up our apartment. I remembered to stop, drop, and roll. I hit the floor and made it to the door.

My neighbor across the street ran to the back room and picked my mother up. I went to their apartment and sat on the couch. They called the ambulance for my mother. I felt guilty because of the way I felt about their family. They saved our lives.

I learned a great lesson on this particular day. My mother was still teaching me in her last days. It was the love some never find in life. Her giving saved our lives. Her love saved our lives. Her compassion saved our lives. Her spirit saved our lives. My mother was sick, but her spirit was strong.

Finally, an apartment opened up about 15 minutes away. We were moving to the Thomas Rolfe apartments. My mother's condition was not improving. Her skin looked like a piece of paper caught on fire. It was brown and black. These spots were all over her body. The spots would bleed. It was only a matter of time before she would die.

Every night, I would give my mother a kiss, hug her and lay her in the bed before she went to sleep. This particular night was different. I tried to get out of the bed two times, but my mother wouldn't let me move. She held me down in the bed. I went to sleep holding her hand. All of a sudden, I felt someone pulling on me. It was a hard pull. I woke up and turned to my mother. Her arms were in the air. She was looking down at her body. Her spirit left her body.

I remember her exact words: "I'm on my way home. It's over."

I really didn't know what really occurred that morning. I woke, gave my mother a kiss and went to school. I remember calling home to check on my mother. She was in a coma. They took her to the hospital. I went back to class.

I was thinking about the last six years of my mother's life. Her smiles, frowns, ups, and downs. The fact that she never said anything bad about my father amazed me. How she would give her last to help the least. Her wet kisses she would give all the time. Her love and compassion for people she didn't know.

I remember how my mother would tell me, "God is going to bless you for taking care of me." I was a little boy becoming a man. My mother stayed in the hospital for a couple of days. I wasn't worried. I was tired of seeing my mother suffer. I was 13 years old. It was becoming unbearable. I wanted it to be over deep down inside.

I recall the phone ringing. It was the hospital. It was about 2:15 in the morning. The doctor called my house. He asked to speak to my grandmother. I took the message. He stated, "please let the family know that Annie Mar Clay has expired."

I called my grandma. I went back to sleep. I woke up the next day happy. I even won something on the radio. It was December, and the weather was tricky. The family planned the funeral. It was going to take place on December 19, 1982. I recall it snowing really hard that day. It was beautiful. It was joyous. My sister and father took it hard. My father never came to check on my mother while she was sick.

I'm glad I apologized to my mother for calling her a b****. A life lesson was learned. When a person is lying in the casket, you remember everything you should have done, could have done, and would have done. You think about everything bad you did to that person. The funeral was my release. It was finally over. I could breathe again. I could be a kid. I could be a witness. The seed was planted to give birth to my calling on earth.

In life, you must reveal to heal. My healing started when I wrote this book. Are you ready to heal?

Why didn't Dr. Clay's mother leave earlier?

_____

_____

_____

_____

Why do parents allow young people to view violence in the home?

_____

_____

_____

_____

How does this chapter relate to you?

_____

_____

_____

_____

How do you really think the writer felt?

_____

_____

_____

_____

What was your greatest takeaway?

_____

_____

_____

_____

What did you learn from this chapter?

_____

_____

_____

_____

Does this chapter relate to someone you know?

_____

_____

_____

_____

CHAPTER 3

The Day I Divorced Religion

"We cannot think of being acceptable to others until we have first proven acceptable to ourselves."

– Malcolm X

I remember growing up with my grandmother. My grandmother was a Christian; she loved the Lord and the pastor. She was a praying woman. She would give her last money to the church. My grandmother had this picture of a white man on the wall. I would walk in the house, and he would look at me. I would say to myself, "Why does my grandmother have a picture of a white man on the wall?" I was scared of this man. I didn't know who he was until one day when she hollered his name. She loved the Messiah.

My typical Sunday was full of food, praise and worship, the reverend, and fried potatoes. My grandmother would be in the kitchen, singing her gospel music and cooking up a storm. We had this old floor radio with turning knobs. You'd better not touch that radio on Sunday. She didn't play on Sunday. On Sunday, she loved the pastor more than she loved me.

I was confused, I mean the reverend couldn't do anything wrong. I never understood how one man could have so much control over a woman. In our house, you couldn't eat until the good reverend finished eating. I was a little boy. You mean to tell me I can't eat until this man comes to my house and eats? He knew he was going to get a nice hot-cooked country meal.

I loved my grandmother, but the reverend was getting on my nerves. He couldn't do anything wrong. She would always talk about the reverend. I felt like he was taking advantage of my grandmother. He would come in, smiling and laughing. His stomach was big. He loved to eat. My grandmother's parents were from North Carolina. Her skills in the kitchen were out of this world.

My grandmother didn't play with church. She made sure we went every Sunday. My grandfather very seldom went to church. He didn't like the reverend or going to church. He never said anything to my grandmother about the reverend. My grandmother was crazy. She was a little woman. My grandfather came in drunk one day, and they fought. She hit him with a frying pan and knocked his teeth out. He was scared of my grandmother, and I was too.

I stayed in the church for several years. We didn't have enough young people, and the choir wasn't good. I loved music with a good beat: the type of music that would make you come out of your seat and move your feet. I guess the choir wasn't good like other churches.

We sat in the back. My grandmother would sit close to the front. She would always find a way to see me. In church, you better not talk, play, or make any noise. We sat in the back and made fun of people. We would make fun of the choir leader. He would move oddly and dance. We would laugh at the woman who would run around the church every Sunday. We thought she was crazy. I can recall talking in church, and my grandmother would give me "The Look." I was done.

In those days, the church was the backbone of the community. If you needed anything, you went to the church. They didn't beg for money. The people would give their money to the church. My grandmother was a giver and then some. I remember the deacons from the church. They were holy men of God. I respected those men because of my grandmother.

I will never forget walking down the King Court stretch one day. A white van pulled up. It was the deacons from the church. They were drinking Budweiser. They were toasted. They wanted us to get in the van. I remember one sticking his hands out and trying to grab me. I pushed back and went home. I never told my grandmother. She wouldn't have believed me over the good old deacons. I saw them the following Sunday. They didn't say a word, and I didn't either.

During my high school years, nothing changed about church. But I remember them telling us that bad people go to Hell and good people go to Heaven. I was scared. I didn't like the word Hell. I wasn't going to Hell. I was going to be a good person. My grandmother told me that if you go out on Saturday, you'd better get up for church. I made sure I got up. I knew if I didn't, the possible consequences would not be to my liking.

I would go to church tired from hanging out with my friends on Saturday. I was scared of Hell. The stories about it in the Bible didn't make it sound like a good place. I was determined to do right in my life. I wanted to make it to Heaven. I became older and continued to attend church. One thing was missing were the men. The leaders of the church were men, and the rest were women.

I remember how the deacons would look at the women during church. We would catch them looking at the backsides of women and whispering. We would watch the deacon leave church with Sister Love. You could see the smirks on their face. I remember one of the Deacons coming to my house. It wasn't for Bible study. I was sitting on the couch. The Deacon was making little comments. He tried to sit close to my grandmother. She put him in check quick. He was lucky he didn't get hit with a frying pan.

We noticed how all the women in the church wanted to be cool with the leaders there. It was like being in the cool clique in school. We knew something was going on after service. It was a lot of extra prayer and laying of hands on certain members. I wouldn't tell my grandmother. My grandmother planted some good seeds in me when it came to loving and caring for people. She planted some good seeds about the life of the Messiah (Yahushua).

I grew older and took some time away from the church. I was tired and wanted something different in my life. My grandmother didn't say anything. She allowed me to live my life. She was always praying for me when I was running the street. I was working, saving money, and enjoying the single life. I finally moved away from home. I shared an apartment with a frat brother from the Phi Beta Sigma Fraternity. You couldn't tell us anything.

We both completed our master's degrees. We were educated, smart, smooth, and loved the ladies. Our weekends started on Thursdays and ended on Sundays. Both of our families were heavy in the church. Our families planted good seeds. We ran the streets for years. Eventually, we got back in church. We started going back because all the ladies were in church. We would go to church and watch the ladies after service. The women in the church were beautiful. It was like the club but a step above the rest.

I remember meeting this woman who was an engineer. She worked at Phillip Morris. I still remember her name today. She was everything a man wanted in a woman. She was older, classy, educated, and down to earth. She was fine as wine. I wasn't ready. I still was running the streets looking for my fantasy.

My roommate moved to Maryland. We stayed in contact. He was attending this church. He would tell me about this church every time we spoke on the phone. He started changing. He was active in the church. He ended up getting a new job. He was making almost $25,000 more than he was previously. He got married, purchased a home, purchased a Toyota 4Runner, became a pastor, and earned his doctorate.

I thought about my grandmother. I thought about the man on the wall. The one my grandmother always talked about and the power of his spirit. It was playing out in front of my eyes. I ended up visiting the church. It was a large church, and the choir was off the hook. The women were beautiful. I couldn't believe it. I eventually moved to Herndon, Virginia. I was closer to Maryland than Richmond. I wanted to be blessed like my roommate. I eventually left Herndon and moved to

Woodbridge. I lived in Woodbridge for three years. I would drive three days a week to church.

I ended up moving to Prince George's County, Maryland. I was looking for a house. I lived in this woman's cold basement while looking for my house. I was going to church. I was working in my career. I was meeting plenty of ladies. I couldn't believe it. I served in the youth ministry. I became the counselor for the Saturday school. It was a paid position. I couldn't believe it.

I stayed in church, serving for 15 years. I saw things I couldn't explain. I had things happen to me I couldn't explain. I was taught things that have helped me greatly. I never thought I would leave the church. This was my family: my home away from home. I made good friends there and still have them today. One in particular is Tonya Dixon. I met her sitting at Door 5 during the weekday. She has been a true friend indeed. She is a Dallas Cowboys fan and loved helping the young girls. She reminds me of my mother.

My decision to divorce my church wasn't easy. I started studying more and searching for a deeper understanding of God. I was seeing the destruction of the family, children, youth, and community. I started having reservations about what I was taught. I started revisiting everything I was taught. I was saved, but what about the people who died before Christ? Why do preachers say you have to give to the church to be blessed? I was going to be cursed if I didn't give money to the church?

Our communities were falling apart. The divorce rate was high. We didn't own anything in our communities. The children were suffering. The parents were crying. My brothers were dying. I would leave church and see homeless people. How could we have these massive buildings when people were suffering in the streets? Why did most pastors live large?

I could quote Marvin Gaye's "What's Going On." Unfortunately, a majority of what I was taught was tradition and not the truth. I started asking God, "Why?"

During this time period, the craziest thing occurred.

I was on the school system's crisis team in my district. Within one week, there were two shootings in my school district. Two young African-American boys were killed. The crisis team had to report to each high school. On both occasions, I was assigned to the young man who was with the boy before he was killed. It was a chilling experience.

I put my skills to the test. It was a battle. I came home and asked God, "Why?" Why all of a sudden were the pastors on TV talking about programs we needed to have in place? Tyrone was shot last week. I didn't hear any pastors talking about programs. This situation was all over the news. They wanted to be part of the story. I decided it was time to leave religion. How can I stay in something when I know it's lying, deceiving, or untruthful?

I'm watching my people suffer. I'm watching children suffer. I'm watching African-Americans suffer. I'm seeing homeless people. Would you stay in a bad relationship, friendship or marriage if something wasn't right and your spirit is pulling you out? It was during this time period that I experienced two major events. I was approached by a member in my church. He wanted me to invest in a social media platform for Christians. It was called Christ-Tube. I thought it was a wonderful idea.

I met with the CEO of the company. His vision was laid out in plain sight. There were retired NFL players who had already invested. There was one NFL player on staff. The office was nice. The people I met were nice. I was quite impressed. I spoke with several of my colleagues, family members, and business friends. They thought it was a great idea. I decided to invest $10,000. I remember him calling me the night before I was scheduled to bring him the check. He stated, "Dr. Clay, I was talking to one of my boys last night, and I thought about you. He reminds me of you."

I spent three years after that waiting on the launch of "Christ-Tube." I would visit the office. He would make all these promises. My church colleagues would follow suit. "Be patient. We are launching next week." I would go the office month after month and excuse after excuse. They were still pushing and pimping Christ.

Upon further research, it turned out I wasn't the only one who was taken in. The NFL player who was part of the staff introduced Christ-

Tube to other players. They invested and lost their money. I remember going to the office one day, and they were using power from the hallway. I don't know if they were given permission to do that. Finally, they were forced to move out. The rent wasn't paid.

This left a bad taste in my mouth about Christianity. How could people who represented Christ mislead, lie, and continue to rip people off? There was a more recent story that broke in Virginia. Here's how NBC's News4 out of Washington, D.C., covered it:

"A senior pastor and his wife defrauded members of their Virginia congregation of more than a million dollars, prosecutors said.

"Victorious Life Church Pastor Terry Wayne Millender; his wife, Brenda; and church member Grenetta Wells — all of Alexandria — were arrested Sunday in a $1.2 million scheme, allegedly operating a company that claimed to help the poor and recruited investors with the false promise of guaranteed return rates, according to an indictment released by the U.S. Attorney's Office of the Eastern District of Virginia.

"The company claimed a Christian mission of providing loans to start or expand existing businesses in developing companies, prosecutors said, but actually used the money for personal reasons, including payments toward the Millenders' $1.75 million home.

"They blamed the Great Recession, among other things, for the delayed repayments, prosecutors said.

"Federal authorities began investigating three years ago when some investors became suspicious."

This shocked me. I started researching more, and things didn't add up! I felt like I was hoodwinked and bamboozled.

During this period, I was scheduled to speak at the Church of Christ's "Save our Sons Summit" on the campus of Virginia State University. Leu Gilbert was the minister of the Arlington Road Church of Christ in Hopewell during this period. We were talking on the phone.

"Minister Leu, I'm not coming down to speak as a therapist or counselor," I told him. "Please make sure you have a counselor available. My topic is going to be heavy."

I spoke for 12 minutes. I noticed this mother and son leave while I was speaking. They got up and walked out of the session. I went back to my table to sell books. There were people lined up, waiting to buy books. I started signing and, all of a sudden, someone ran up to the table.

"Dr. Clay, we need you in the room! A mother and son are breaking down in the front."

My heart couldn't allow me to leave them in an emotional state of peril. I went in like a counselor. It was broader than counseling; this was spiritual warfare. I didn't realize how deep it was until I got into the battle. This went on for 30 minutes. This young man and his mother were emotionally incarcerated. It was years and years of incarceration for both of them together. They wore me out. I was tired. I remember falling asleep.

It was 3:00 in the morning. My phone rang, and the spirit said *the person on the line is going to tell you you're going to die tomorrow.*

Okay. Yeah right, I'm saying to myself. I played the voicemail back. The message was exact. The message said, "Tomorrow, you're going to die. I'm going to kill you tomorrow." I was scared. I kept playing the message over and over. I went back to sleep. I got up and was looking out the window. I called the police. They thought someone was playing a prank. They thought I made someone mad.

I called Verizon. They couldn't trace it because I didn't answer the phone. I went to church the next day. I shared the message with the panel. They were shocked. I was still looking over my back. I had to drive three hours back home. It felt like six hours. I was watching every car around me on the highway. I made it back to Maryland safe. I was still looking around for a couple of days.

I went to pull up my website. My website was down. I was scheduled to speak on Thursday. I didn't believe it. I was upset. I called my webmaster, and he couldn't explain. He came up with all these excuses. I called the hosting company, and they couldn't explain. This went on for days. I eventually told my webmaster he was fired. I was done dealing with him. I ended up meeting someone from outside the country online. He created a new website.

I gave birth to Boysoffthehook.com. I thought over this situation for days. My old website wasn't a reflection of my knowledge, skills, and abilities. My new website was a true reflection of the gift I was born to share with the world.

The transition has not been smooth. I was married to religion my whole life. It was my foundation. My grandmother was a Christian. A majority of my friends are Christians. My family members are Christians. My whole life was based around Christianity. The Most High has always been the rock of my foundation.

My flesh started questioning my decision to leave. This would be a lonely journey. I didn't know what would happen in my life. My emotions were running and ramped up. All my friends were in the church. How would they respond? Who would I hang out with? How would my family respond? Would people think I was strange? There are 7.5 billion people in the world, and this way was the only way?

After reflecting on my religion growing up, could I find truth within those realms? Why did I look at other people in other religions differently? Who taught me this way of life? Why was my way the only way to Heaven? Why was Jesus white? Why did my grandmother have this white man on the mall? Why was he my savior? Did I become a Christian because of my family? Why was I here? Why was everybody else who didn't believe going to Hell?

It was painful, but self-reflection is good for cleansing. I needed clarification. I received it! It was "cognitive dissonance."

What is cognitive dissonance? The term is used to describe the *feeling of discomfort* that results from holding two conflicting beliefs. When there is an inconsistency between belief and behavior, something must change to eliminate or reduce the dissonance. In other words, this happens when you find out something that goes entirely against what you were taught.

What was my purpose, and was I truly walking in my purpose? I knew that, in order to reach the inner part of my soul, something had to die. I would have to be born again. I would have to tap into the inner me – a place called Pineal – a higher level of consciousness. I allowed my spirit to guide me to peace and understanding. In essence, I could no longer box myself into one system of belief.

Achieving a higher level of consciousness requires change. My goal was to impact humanity. My goal wasn't to impact religion. I'm sure you might not agree with my stance; however, I will hope you're able to put your beliefs aside and look at the bigger picture.

We're all human beings striving to find peace, love, and purpose. My life purpose was not to be a judge, football player, lawyer, or airline pilot. Those are careers with which you can express your purpose. Your life purpose is more about who you are at your core and what you are here to learn and give than it is about what you do for a living. You need to know where you're going in life. It's vital that you have an identity.

I've been called to change lives. What about you? Are you missing out on your calling? What is your purpose? What are you passionate about? I am passionate about helping children and families in need. Can I walk into that purpose if I box myself into believing that my way is the only way? Can I impact humanity being selfish?

How do I determine my purpose? I wake up every day on purpose. I sleep with purpose. I eat with purpose. I speak with purpose. I think with purpose. I wake up with purpose. I praise with purpose. I counsel with purpose. I am purpose.

I sleep with passion. I wake up with passion. I eat with passion. I speak with passion. I think with passion. I counsel with passion. I praise with passion. I am passion.

I wake up with peace of mind. I sleep with peace of mind. I eat with peace of mind. I praise with peace of mind. I counsel with peace of mind. I am peace of mind.

I know you're saying, "Dr. Clay, it sounds good, but what are the steps to determining your purpose?" The first step: You have to speak those things as though life and death are on your tongue. The second step: Start speaking positively. The third step: Eliminate all negative energy. The fourth step: Write down what you're passionate about and define your "why"? Finally: Pray! Ask yourself, can your "why" lead to purpose, passion, and peace of mind?

Create a list and work toward it, and remember that quitting is not an option. People are waiting for your purpose and passion. It's time to live your life. You must create a roadmap to life. You were called, and you know where you're going. Nothing can stop you. Don't allow discouragement to distract you permanently. Your past won't dictate your future. You have been called to do something big because your purpose is huge. You're reading this book because the Most High want's to free you from your emotional incarceration.

Remember: The only person that can stop you is you. You are passion and purpose. And no one else determines your destiny but you! You must find the answer within! You were created in the image of the creator.

We must see people as humans, not as cultures or belief systems. This will hinder your growth as a human being when you stop allowing yourself to grow out of the confines of your belief system. You were born a spirit and will die a spirit. It's my mandate to write in spirit and in truth.

For the record, I'm not in the business of changing one's belief system. Every person walking the earth has to search within themselves to find a belief system that serves as their gateway to peace of mind. This is my story. Regardless of who you serve or what you believe, we're all human beings. It's time we put our differences aside and serve humanity with love, passion, and conviction.

I divorced religion. I'm married to me. I no longer look outside of me for answers! I was created in the image of Yah. The kingdom of heaven is within.

I will close with this quote by Debasish Mridha: "Deep love for humanity is a vaccine for depression."

What was your greatest takeaway?

_____

_____

_____

_____

Why are we so divided?

_____

_____

_____

_____

Why did the author write this chapter?

_____

_____

_____

_____

Did you ever question what you're taught?

_____

_____

_____

_____

Isn't love the greatest vehicle to mankind?

_____

_____

_____

_____

What did you learn from this chapter?

_____

_____

_____

_____

How did this chapter relate to you?

_____

_____

_____

_____

CHAPTER 4

Man Down: Father Gone

"The human father has to be confronted and recognized as human, a man who created a child and then, by his absence, left the child fatherless and then godless."

– Anaias Nin

One of the greatest challenges facing young children today is growing up fatherless. There is no question that children who grow up in fatherless homes have a much greater risk of major challenges in life than those who grow up with a father at home. We might want to believe otherwise, and sometimes political correctness causes us to want to think otherwise. But the truth is that fathers matter.

In the United States, there are 9 million black families, and the divorce rate is around 50%. Furthermore, in the black family today, at least 63% of boys are raised by single mothers (4).

Early research portrayed African-American fathers as generally absent or uninvolved in their children's lives (5). In contrast, more recent findings on African-American fathers paint a different picture. This research shows that African-American fathers, across socioeconomic and residency statuses, are involved with and interested in their children, and can be nurturing and sensitive to their needs (6). Studies of resident fathers show that, compared to white fathers, African-Americans spend equivalent time in direct activities with their children and monitor their children more (7).

Other, more nuanced findings show that fathers spend less time with their children during the week than during the weekend; and black fathers have been found to spend more time on weekends relative to white fathers (7). The total amount of time spent with children and how it's divided across the days of the week may be less significant for children's outcomes than the sensitivity and responsiveness of fathers during their time together (7). Unfortunately, one of the most significant challenges facing America today is the lack of fathers in the lives of their children.

I never really knew my father growing up. I recall growing up in a nice house. I remember my father working and coming home. I remember sitting on the porch and watching him come home from work. I remember standing in the doorway and watching him wash the cars. I don't recall ever really having a father and son moment. It was something I wanted growing up, but I don't recall having that special moment.

If I had to describe my relationship with my father growing up, I couldn't. I don't recall him ever coming to school when we were living as a family. I would see other parents together, but my father wasn't seen. It was a painful feeling growing up, wanting a relationship with your father but never really being able to develop one.

Everyone in my neighborhood lived with both parents. We all played with each other daily. I remember those days. My father never taught me how to fight, but he would fight my mother. I remember liking this girl in third grade. Her name was Kimberly Winfield. I would sit in lunch and watch her. She was funny and cool. I wanted a girlfriend. I wanted Kimberly.

I wrote her a letter. I wanted to be her boyfriend. She said no. I was hurt. I stopped going to lunch. All my friends knew how much I like Kim.

She showed everyone the letter. I was ashamed. I wish my father would have been around more to help me. I remember one night; my father whipped me for something stupid. He really put a whipping on me. He would talk to me while beating me. I could see years of anger in his eyes. His abuse became normal to me. I grew up scared to say the wrong thing. It would lead to a whipping. I went through my childhood in terror.

I never really knew what to expect from my father. I remember waking up and going into the kitchen to get breakfast. My father was sitting in the family room, happily eating pancakes and bacon. My sister was sitting right beside him. I was still mad. I was going to get my father back from those whippings. My father was eating and happy. I walked passed and farted right on his food. I turned around like it slipped out. He was mad. I told him I was going to the bathroom. He got up and dumped his plate, and I laughed all the way to the bathroom. My mother thought it was funny.

I remember being picked on by this boy up the street. He would beat me up every day after school. I told my father, but he never did anything about it. It really bothered me growing up. It was like I didn't have a father in the house. My father was mean. I would get beatings for the smallest thing. He didn't waste time pulling out the belt. I never saw him give my sister a beating, but he tore me up.

I do recall this one particular week. I remember hanging out with my friends around the street. We were smoking cigarettes. I was choking trying to smoke cigarettes. I decided I would take some cigarettes home and practice. I knew my father didn't get home until five, so I was good. I was in the basement. I pulled out the cigarette, lit it up and began to walk up the steps. I looked up, and there was my father. I almost swallowed the cigarette. I finally thought my father cared for me. He didn't want me smoking. He said it would kill me. My father beat another hole in me the same day. I don't smoke today.

Finally, my father showed how much he cared. Any sense of caring from my father was good news to me. We continued to live in the nice house. The relationship between my parents was reckless; my relationship with my father wasn't any better. My mother couldn't do too much because he would snap for the least little thing. I felt like my father would take out his anger on me because I was close to my mother. I was mama's boy, and my sister was daddy's girl.

My mother never showed a difference in how she felt about my sister and I. This was mindblowing growing up. I thought parents loved their children equally. I never stopped trying to be a good son to my father, but he didn't seem to care. I wanted my father to be proud of me. We continued to live in our house, and my father produced another son outside of marriage. My mother was hurt. I was shocked. I wanted to see how much time he would spend with my brother. My stepbrother was named Bobby.

My brother eventually received the same treatment. However, because my father wasn't present, he was abused. My father was upset because his son was gay. He stopped communication with him. My brother's nickname was "Skip," and mine was "Flip." My father never brought his name up in conversation. He was ashamed. My father didn't have anything to do with my brother. He basically disowned my brother. The cycle continued like water flowing down the stream. My brother ended up suffering from depression. He doesn't leave his house and can't function in public.

Meanwhile, I knew the marriage was over. My mother didn't leave, and I couldn't believe it. Finally, my father lost his mind. He was upset with my mother. He picked up the phone, threw it, and knocked her eye out of place. She was rushed to the hospital. A couple of days later, my mother left. I knew for a fact that I wouldn't see my father for a while. We moved right up the street to an apartment. We stayed one year. My mother became sick. My parents finally divorced. My sister decided to live with my father, and I went with my mother. We moved about 20 minutes away. My mother died four years later. I ended up living with my grandmother.

My father very seldom picked up the phone to contact me. We eventually spoke on the phone. I wanted to see my father. I was excited. My father told me he was going to pick me up on Friday. I would pack my clothes on Thursday. He promised me for two years. I don't recall him ever picking me up more than five times. I would sit on the porch and wait for him. I remember seeing his car. I couldn't believe it! He pulled up. He said, "Junior, an emergency came up." He apologized and drove off. I was tired and hurt. I still kept the faith. I spoke to him on Thursday night.

I will never forget this conversation. He promised he would be there on Friday. I waited and waited. He never showed up. My grandmother didn't say anything. I'd lost my mother. I didn't have my father. He would eventually come by the house to bring me money. I wanted his presence, not his presents. I took what I could get from him. Our relationship was over the phone. I very seldom saw my father, his physical absence stretching out for months at a time. He never came to any of my school events. He never came to any meetings. He didn't know any of my teachers. He didn't even know my grades.

I'm 14 years old and hurting. I went to school every day. You couldn't tell I was in pain. I was happy in school. This was one place I could go and forget about my problems. I was very popular in school. I was the manager of the football, basketball, and baseball teams. The coaches became my stepfathers. The players became my brothers.

I earned the name "Flip" while riding on the bus from a football game. We were always cracking jokes after we won a game. I recall coming back from a win, and I was joking on this particular player. I was flowing, and the whole bus was laughing. One of the players yelled out, "You're crazy like Flip Wilson. I'm going to call you Flip." My father never knew how I became Flip! It's certain moments in a child's life where the lack of a father hurts more.

My days were long. My days were sad. My days were like night and day. I maintained my hope in my father; however, other days, I really didn't care what happened. I was losing hope! I would go in my room and cry thinking about what I did wrong. His problem was my fault. I graduated from high school. I don't recall my father coming to my graduation. I was a grown emotionally incarcerated young man.

I decided to attend Charleston Job Corps in Charleston, West Virginia. I wanted to get away! I was doing very well at Job Corps. My father would send me money every blue moon. He was cheap. He would send me five dollars here or 10 dollars there. I begged to get the money. I couldn't understand why he was so cheap. He made good money.

His issue was all his women. I remember calling home. I needed some money. He told me, "I'm going to send you 10 dollars on Friday." The money came in the mail. It was a $100.00 money order. I called my father, so excited.

I said, "Thanks, Dad! I really appreciate it."

He said, "You deserved it. I'm proud of you."

I spoke to my sister a couple weeks later. We were talking on the phone. She asked me about the money. She said the lady at the post office made a mistake on the money order. She added another zero to the money order. My father decided to keep the money order and send it to me. I didn't know what to think. He was lying or stretching the truth?

My sister was in college during this time period. She eventually graduated from Norfolk State University. My father was happy. He was a proud father. His baby girl graduated. I'm still tripping because he didn't say anything about the money order? I don't know why I would expect more from him. Regardless, he was still my father. I know he lied in the past, but I wanted to give him the benefit of the doubt.

I ended up graduating from West Virginia State University. I transferred to Virginia State University and completed my master's degree. My father was finally proud of me. We were in the kitchen talking one day. I will never forget what came out of his mouth.

"I'm proud of you, son. I never thought you would do better than your sister."

I'm thinking to myself, this man is crazy. I believed in my father. I was the spitting image of my mother. The compassion, love, peace, and understanding for my father would never end. Our relationship became stronger over time.

My grandmother who raised me passed. I purchased the house from all the family members. The city wanted the property. I refused to allow the city to purchase the house. That meant I had to deal with the city.

"Sir, you know it's going to cost over $50,000 dollars to remodel the house. The taxes are past due. How soon can you pay the taxes?"

I handled my business the same day. I spoke to my father. "I'm thinking about fixing Grandma's house up." He was very supportive. I told him what occurred when dealing with the city. He just smiled.

I was living in Maryland. I'm working on my doctoral degree, working full time and speaking. My father was instrumental in helping me complete the project. He handled the money. He would drive down and check on the house. He made sure everybody was in place. He was finally my father. We were riding in the truck one day, leaving the house.

My father stated, "I made some mistakes growing up, and I hope you understand? I wish I would have done things different."

He never said he was sorry. I was glad he saw the error of his ways. I ended up totally rehabbing the house. I remember my father walking through the house. He would tell me stories of how my grandmother (Ms. Edith) took him in when he got out of the Army. He told me if it wasn't for Ms. Edith, he would have never made it in life.

I could see the transformation. He was finally sharing. He was finally showing his emotion. He was my father. It took me six years to complete my doctoral degree. My father told all his friends, "My son is going to be a doctor." He would brag to everybody. My father came to my graduation. He took pictures. He took extra copies of the program. Our relationship was better than ever.

I decided I want to write a book. I wanted to help other young men overcome the various obstacles and challenges in life. My father was very supportive. I wrote my first book. The book was titled *Post-Traumatic School Disorder: Empowerment Strategies for African-American Males.* I gave my father a copy. He started reading the book. He became highly upset. He stopped talking to me. His pride was shaken. He told the world about his son becoming a doctor. However, he never told the world about his role of not being a father. I told the secret. I shared the dirty laundry. I didn't share all of it, but enough.

My father was mad. He stopped talking to me. I went back to my childhood. My father was repeating the same cycle again. He stopped being my father.

My sister called and said, "You need to call your father."

"If he is upset, it's because I told the truth!" I meant every word I said and hung up the phone.

My father and I didn't talk for months. I put it in the Most High's hands. I was done with him. It was the first week in December, and my phone rang. It was my father. I was shocked because he wanted five copies of the book. He even wanted to pay for them. I didn't ask any questions. A couple of weeks later, I gave my father the books. He and I were sitting on the back porch talking about the Bible, life, and being thankful.

My father started going to church and reading the Bible more. He loved Dr. Fred Price. He would send money to the ministry all the time. This particular night, we talked about his childhood. His father wasn't in his life growing up. He never really knew his father. You could see the pain in his eyes. His mother was very promiscuous, and it bothered him deep down inside. My father also spoke about how proud my mother would be of me if she was alive. He kept up with my mother's age. I'm glad my father was able to release. My father wasn't going to leave this earth emotionally incarcerated. It's beautiful to watch men tap into their innermost self to heal.

My father told me he wasn't feeling well. I told him to make an appointment to see the doctor. He continued having health issues, but he hated going to the doctor. He shared with me that he was still having health issues, but I knew he would be fine. I remember seeing my father for the last time. He didn't look the same. He barely could walk and didn't seem like himself. I told my sister to keep me posted on his health. My sister would call me to keep me posted.

I remember driving back to Maryland and thinking about how he was looking. I was happy our relationship was better. My sister called me worried about my father. He wouldn't go to the doctor, and his health was getting worse. We talked on the phone, and he promised me he would go to the doctor again on Monday. My sister called me and stated that Dad was in the hospital. My father never made it to Monday. He died a couple of days later. I couldn't believe it. We were just talking on the phone three days earlier.

After his death, I started reflecting on our relationship. Our conversations before he died helped me to understand him better. I was ha thankful. My father wanted a small funeral. My stepbrother didn't attend the funeral. He was buried with his Dallas Cowboys paraphernalia. He loved the Cowboys, and so do I. I'm glad I had the opportunity to "dance with my father" before he died.

The new ideal of "man down, father gone" hit home! He was gone. The solution to fatherlessness, morality, immorality, and broken families is compassion, truthfulness, love, faith, commitment, and a relationship with God. They are available to each of us. However, only we can make the choice to be great fathers and parents. One real challenge is teaching the value of family. This starts with each of us.

For nearly half of Americans, Father's Day is really "fatherless day." The reality is that too many kids don't have real fathers. They don't have men of honor, love, conviction, and principle in their lives. However, increasingly, good dads aren't hard to find. I want to say Thank You to the one million plus single fathers who are dancing with their child or children.

Why do you think the author wrote this chapter?

_____

_____

_____

_____

Why are so many fathers missing?

_____

_____

_____

_____

Do you know someone who needs to read this chapter?

_____

_____

_____

Why is it so hard for people to discuss this issue?

Do you have hope in your father?

What did you learn from this chapter?

How did this chapter relate to you?

What was your greatest takeaway?

Are you ready to forgive?

CHAPTER 5

Emotional Detoxification

*"Nobody ever really knows how much someone else
is hurting. We could be standing next to someone
who feels broken, and we wouldn't know it."*

– Dr. Sun Wolf

The role of counselor can be emotionally draining. Can you imagine listening to problems every day? You're the one people always seek for help.

My journey started in schools and churches, and ended up working with males of all ages. I can recall my first job after completing my master's degree. I completed college in December and was hired the following January to work in a predominately white school district in Northern Virginia as an elementary school counselor.

As an elementary school counselor, I felt like I could make a difference because of what I went through as a child. I was an itinerate counselor assisting the school-based counselors with their duties across four schools. I loved the idea of going to four different schools and meeting the various parents, students, and teachers there. It seemed to me that every teacher wanted me to speak with all the boys, especially black boys. I felt like a star.

My success came from the fact that I was energetic, crazy, creative, down-to-earth, and funny, and I spoke to the kids on their level. I've always had a passion for helping children, especially young brothers. Teachers would always ask, "What did you say to them? They have changed their behavior!" I didn't do anything special; I was just myself.

The greatest challenge in life is finding out your purpose. The purpose of who, what, when, and why I was created to be? Can you imagine getting up every day with a sense of purpose? Your parents don't determine your purpose. Your significant other does not determine your purpose. You determine the outcome of your life. I have concluded that whether we enjoy our careers often boils down to how our calling fits with our sense of purpose. Once we find out what we're called to do, life becomes fulfilling. Having a sense of purpose has been critical to my well-being. A sense of purpose motivates me every day and moment.

I recall sitting in my office. It was time to go into the classroom and introduce myself to my students. I entered the classroom and my spirit said, "Tell it all, Dr. Clay." I spent two weeks sharing my life with 13- and 14-year-old students. It was rough. I remember going into this one particular class and talking about my mother. I could see the eyes of the students. I started crying thinking about everything in my life. They were amazed I was so transparent.

The year progressed, and my students would bring up my story. It was Emotional Detoxification 400. I allowed the spirit to guide me into all truth. Those two weeks set the tone for the next two years. I knew students without fathers were major. My students would share with me their stories in my office. It became overwhelming at times.

I recall Tina walking into my office. Tina was 13 and very tall for her age. She was about five-foot eight-inches and 200 pounds. She was a very smart girl, but she would go off in a second. Her mother was dealing with health issues. Her father was in another state. Her father pretty much didn't care about her. Tina sat in the chair and broke down. She hated herself. She blamed herself. She disliked everyone who didn't agree with her. For the next 15 minutes, the tears were falling. I allowed her to release.

After releasing, I defined self-reflection. I pulled out a piece of paper. I wrote down four words. I wrote the words "problem," "cause," "solution," and "implementation." We applied each word to her situation.

What was the problem? Her father was not present in her life.

What was the cause? We had to figure that out.

What was the solution? This was based on the cause.

What was the proper implementation? Whatever Tina was willing to do to bring closure.

Tina and I continued with the conversation. I shared with her how most of our fathers didn't have fathers in their life growing up.

She was shocked. "How about your father?"

I shared the analogy of studying for a test. "If you study for a test, you will probably do very well on the test, correct?"

She said, "Yes, Dr. Clay."

"Your father didn't prepare for the test of being a father. His father never taught him."

She looked amazed. "You really think so, Dr. Clay?"

"Yes!" I told Tina to call her father when she got home. "During the conversation, say, 'Dad, can I ask you a question?' I want you to ask your father if his father was there for him growing up, and then listen for his response."

Tina walked into my office the very next day. "Dr. Clay, can I speak with you?"

"Sure. What's good, Tina?"

"I called my father. I did everything you told me to."

"How was the conversation?

"It was okay until I asked about his father being in his life growing up. The phone became silent. He never said anything. I waited but eventually hung the phone up."

"Tina, can you define the problem?"

"Yes!"

We continued to talk until it was time for class. We would discuss the solution at another time.

It was time for Men Make a Difference Day. This event occurs every year. We invite fathers to school for a day. The day consists of food, speakers, tours, and interaction with the staff. The program consisted of speakers and two assemblies. We conducted one assembly for the girls and one for the boys.

I knew this program would have to be powerful. I was dealing with some serious father issues on my caseload. During the program, we watched a video titled "Found Dead." It was about a father searching for his daughter after years of being absent. The speaker spoke after the video. After the speaker, we watched the video *Dance with My Father* by Luther Vandross. The girls became very emotional. They were crying all over the school – in the hallway, office, classroom, and counselor's office. The school went into crisis mode. It was a very moving experience.

I recall walking into my office, and there were 20 girls waiting for me in tears. I was going crazy. The program was proceeding, and my students needed counseling. I calmed the girls down and developed a group called The Daughters of Destiny. The remainder of the year, more girls and boys wanted to talk about the lack of fathers in their lives. The boys were more secretive with their emotions, but the girls let it out. I spent the rest of the year working hand in hand with all those students.

It was a very overwhelming experience. I started having health issues. There were other variables that weren't helping the problem. My blood pressure was up, and I was continually having chest pains. I went to see a cardiologist. He ran all kinds of test. He didn't find anything. He saw something, but he didn't know what it was. I was confused. He put me on blood pressure pills. The stress was becoming too much to handle. I couldn't figure out. I came back home, and the spirit said, *let it go, Dr. Clay.*

What was inside of me? Those other variables were hindering my healing. I eventually let it go, and my problems were solved. The school year proceeded, and our school district was shocked with the arrest of a teacher's assistant. He was arrested and charged with over 100 state charges, and pleaded guilty to 15 federal counts. He was charged with engaging in sexual activity with minors, using cellphones to record the acts, and more.

The school district went into lockdown mode. If we saw or heard anything, we were mandated to report it. A student, Becky, reported to another student that her stepfather had raped her every weekend for months. They called the student to the office. She wouldn't open up and share her story. She didn't deny it but was scared, hurt, and angry. They were in a dilemma. She wouldn't speak to the police, school security, or anyone else. One of the school security offices knew I was previously on the crisis team before becoming part of the leadership team in the school district. He knew my skills to deal with these issues. He recommended they call me.

I recall sitting in my office. A call came in from the main office. "Dr. Clay, we need you in the main office right away." I walked into the main office and the police, school security, administrators, and parent liaison were all present. I recall everyone's eyes on me when I walked into the room.

"Dr. Clay, we tried. But she will not budge."

I knew exactly what I was going to do. They gave me the details and shared with me where the student was located. I shared with the team that I need thirty minutes. I went to the room. I saw the student. I sat down beside her and made sure she was okay. She was scared and sitting there in a daze. I recommended we walk down to my office and watch videos on YouTube.

We proceeded to walk down the hall and, during our conversation; I asked her if she recalled my story growing up.

She said, "Yes, I remember what you said, Dr. Clay."

She saw one of her friends and started smiling. She sat down in the chair. We chatted for about 15 minutes. I shared with her that I was going to step out of the office.

"I want you to watch this video, and we will talk about it when I return."

She was sitting about nine feet from the screen. I pulled up "Runaway Love" by Mary J. Blige and Ludacris. I hit play and stepped out of the room. I returned 10 minutes later. Her chair was moved up close to the screen. She was in deep thought. The video triggered details of her nightmare. I pulled out my book, *Post-Traumatic School Disorder*, and followed the script.

- How old was Lisa?
- Who didn't believe her?
- Why did she say "Ouch"?
- How did you feel after hearing this song?
- How old is Nicole?
- What did her father do to her?
- Why did they want to run away?

I continued to follow the script. It was done in 30 minutes. I returned back to the office and walked into room. I shared with the team the details. I couldn't believe what this young girl had gone through for nine months. The special operations division was called to take her statement. I sat in the office with her while they took her statement. She didn't want to talk without my presence.

The stepfather was arrested the same day if I recall correctly. The mother was called, and she couldn't believe it at first. I remember her crying on the phone. She arrived at the school mad, angry, upset, and confused. The police were in the room with the mother and little girl. I went back into the conference room to report to the team.

One of the members from school security said, "Dr. Clay, you saved her life."

I stated, "I'm just a vessel doing what Yah called me to do."

I went back to work. The next five months were life-changing. She returned two days later. I spent 70% of my time helping her for the remainder of the year. She wouldn't talk to anybody. She would break down in class. She would start shaking all of a sudden. She would start crying at the blink of an eye. She would sit in class in a daze. She spent months blaming herself. She wanted to cut herself. She wanted to kill herself. She would talk about taking pills to get it over with because of the pain. It was becoming unbearable.

I was back in the doctor's office, but I was determined to stand by her.

My father left me. I thought about everything she disclosed to me, and I couldn't give up. Finally, I decided she needed a support system. I introduced her to my Daughters of Destiny girls group. There were several girls who could relate to her story. She became friends with two girls in particular. They became her support system. They became my support system. We were a tight family. The student and I continued to meet one on one. I promised her I would be there to the end, even if it meant going to court.

She wasn't ready for counseling three months after the incident. Finally, she told me she was ready and started seeing a counselor outside of the school. She finally was making progress. It was the last month of the school year, and everyone noticed the progress. Several staff members even complimented me on the difference in her overall.

"Dr. Clay, you changed her life."

I was making plans not to return the next school year, as there were some people who were not happy with my relationship with the students. I couldn't believe it, and I deserved better. The student and I were talking in my office. She wanted to know what was I going to do over the summer and whether I was returning next year. I told her that I wasn't planning on returning. She wanted to know why.

She said, "The kids like you. The parents like you. Why wouldn't you come back, Dr. Clay?"

"I don't plan on it, but you will be the first to know if anything changes," I told her.

I came home and decided to pray. My prayer was that if she wrote me a note asking me to stay, I would stay. It was a few days before school was out.

She said, "Dr. Clay, I have something for you. I will bring it tomorrow."

I was like, "Cool."

The next morning, she handed me a note. It was written in cursive. The note read:

> Thank you for being one of the greatest role models.
> Thank you for helping me with my troubles. You truly
> have changed my life. I've always looked at the bad

side, but because of you, I try to look at the good side no matter what. You're the best guidance counselor to ever live. Not only have you changed my life, you've changed others'. We're all grateful for that. Thank you for being the best person to change our lives. Thank you so much for believing in me when I couldn't believe in myself. Thank you so much.

I read this note and started to cry. I had to get myself together. A week later, it was the end of the school year. She wanted to know if I was returning. How could I say no after reading the letter? I decided to return. I wanted to keep my promise. I didn't want to be like my father. I contacted the mother because I wanted to stay in contact with her over the summer through text and on the phone as needed. I knew it was imperative that she maintain the progress she'd made. The mother didn't have a problem with me checking on her daughter to maintain her progress.

I was in church one Sunday. The spirit spoke to me. I sent her a text right before church. I said, "God loves you."

She responded with, "I'm ready to kill myself. My mother and I were having a disagreement. I can't take it no more. Please call me."

I called her and de-escalated the situation. I called Child Protective Services. A month passed, and I would check bi-weekly through text. She was doing fine. I received another text two weeks later. Her brother pushed her to the edge. She was ready to end it again. I called her again to de-escalate the situation.

We returned back to school, and the school system was being sued because of the teacher's assistant who raped and molested several kids. The school district wasn't playing any games. If you heard, saw, or knew anything, you'd better report it. The only contact allowed was high-fives. The doors would be open during all counseling sessions, and counselors would meet with three or more students at a time unless it was urgent. You couldn't run up on the staff and give hugs.

The second week, I saw the crew from my empowerment group. I shared with them the new rules. We shared the rules with the whole school. A week later, Becky's brother threatened to commit suicide. I had to call Child Protective Services. He was in my office. I called his sister down to the office. We contacted the mother. She explained to the mother what occurred.

Her brother said, "Dr. Clay, my sister sees you like a father."

I said, "Please don't say that word. I could get in trouble."

His sister said, "Dr. Clay, don't worry about what people think."

I said, "Please don't say that word. Please."

She was upset. She didn't understand the ramifications. I sent her back to class. A large percentage of my students are from low-income families. My school qualified for Free And Reduced Meal (FARMS). In essence, over 50% of my students lived in poverty. A good male educator becomes a father figure to students who don't have a father in their lives. A majority of them are raised by single parents. They don't see positive male role models all the time.

A couple of hours later, the secretary called me to the principal's office. The teacher reported to the principal that she was upset because I told her she shouldn't say the word "father." She also told the teacher that I was checking up on her over the summer through text messages. The teacher ran to the principal and reported what was stated to her. I was sent home! I couldn't have any contact with any students from my school. I couldn't attend any school system events.

I couldn't believe it. I was under investigation for sending a child text messages that saved her life. There were certain people dragging my name through the gutter around school. They were trying to paint a certain picture without knowing the details. I was out a month and a half, and I received this text message. She was having thoughts of suicide again. She couldn't get in touch with her counselor. She needed guidance.

I couldn't contact her directly. I called the parent liaison. She called the student, and we conducted a three-way. I was able to talk her down. I immediately sent an email message to all parties. It was rough being investigated for text messages that saved a child's life. I was still dealing with my health. I became angry, hurt, and upset. I was thinking about suicide. I wanted it to be over. I was tired. I was ready to end my life.

I reached out to a very close friend, Dr. Sonya Ford, and another person. I shared my thoughts with my supervisor. I came back to reality. I didn't have anything to hide. The text messages spoke for themselves. The evidence was right in their faces. I received a call from the school secretary.

"Dr. Clay, you have a subpoena waiting for you in the office."

I was the main witness for the state. I ended up going to court twice. This was my first time actually sitting in a court as the main witness. The door opened up, and her stepfather came out in cuffs. She jumped and started to cry. Her mother grabbed her to keep her calm. The state attorney started reading information pertaining to the case. I was shocked to hear my name. A professional school counselor was the main reason we were in court today.

She told the judge, "Without the dedication of Dr. William Clay, we wouldn't be here today. She shared the detailed facts of rape to Dr. Clay on that particular day."

We were sitting in court, and this man in front of me kept turning around, looking and whispering. I didn't know what was wrong.

Finally, the gentleman stated, "Dr. Clay, I read your book. It was a great book."

We shook hands, and I thanked him. We went back to court thirty days later for sentencing. The step-father took a plea deal. He was sentenced to seven years. I went back to work two weeks later. I was never questioned why I was under investigation. I knew certain people were trying to paint a picture without knowing the facts. My real friends shared with me who the culprits were. We were having a staff meeting. I shared the truth and shut it down. My principal put the butter on the popcorn. He reminded the staff how I went outside my duty hours to save a child's life. My haters were looking bamboozled.

I returned back to work. I was glad to be back. Furthermore, that same student would stop by my office several days a week at 11:00 during lunch. She wanted to help me with everything. She became a big sister to other girls in the school. She would share with them how much of a difference I made in her life. She would share with them her story.

She was 100% better. I was so proud of her progress. I'm happy to report that the young lady went on to high school. She is still in counseling. She is no longer depressed. She is no longer on medication. Her grades have improved. Her counselor stated she is doing well.

I would love for a corporation or someone with the finances to send her to college. I thought about setting up a GoFundMe. I would love to present her with a check or free ticket to college – a check that will cover her college cost. This would truly change her life. I'm sure that someone reading this book will know somebody who can make this happen. Furthermore, if you would like to take the lead in helping this young lady go to college, please contact me. She truly changed my life. This is the least I can do.

I will close with this: The life of a counselor can be life-changing. The stress behind listening to problems can be overwhelming. Black male mental health professionals need time to release. We need time to detox. We need people to listen to us. This period in my professional career defined me. It validated my purpose of living. It was my emotional detoxification.

What was your greatest takeaway?

_____

_____

_____

_____

How do you feel about Tina?

_____

_____

_____

_____

How do you feel about Becky?

_____

_____

_____

_____

Why do think the author was feeling so depressed?

_____

_____

_____

_____

Why was Tina's father silent?

_____

_____

_____

_____

What did you learn from this chapter?

_____

_____

_____

_____

How did this chapter relate to you?

_____

_____

_____

_____

CHAPTER 6

Love, Lies, and Emotions

"When a man is prey to his emotions, he is not his own master."

— Baruch Spinoza

I graduated from high school. My grades weren't good. I wasn't thinking about college. I wanted to get a job and help my grandmother. She took me in after my mother died. I didn't want to live with my father. He didn't have the time. I knew if he hadn't come around to see my mother, he wouldn't have time for me.

I started working with temp agencies. I purchased a car. My grandmother never took my money. She told me to save my money. I finally was hired. I was working for the government. My job was 15 minutes from my house. I was doing very well. I was making money, and everything was good. I left the government job and was hired as a sanitation control worker. I was working at a Food Lion warehouse. I was really making good money. I worked there for five years. Meanwhile, my cousin Monte Drew left for Job Corps. He returned home and told me about Charleston Job Corps.

I was making good money, but I was missing something. This something couldn't be found in my hometown. I decided to quit my job and further my education. All my friends said I was crazy.

"You are going to quit your job and go to Job Corps? You are a fool."

I started having second thoughts. I decided to leave. I decided to attend Charleston Job Corps. It took a long time to get in. Charleston Job Corps was the Harvard, Hampton, Yale, or Howard of Job Corps. Charleston was so unique because it was in the middle of downtown Charleston, West Virginia. You could go to college for free. Finally, there were so many girls, it was sickening.

This old hotel was converted to a Job Corps residence. I think the center contained six to eight floors. One floor was all boys. My floor was co-ed. The rest of the floors were all women. My cousin was on point. I was in heaven. I left right before Thanksgiving and didn't want to come home for Christmas. I needed to get away. I was still having my "I miss my mother" days. I was having a good time, but I started getting lonely. After being in the center and behaving well, you could earn a weekend pass. I was earning passes but didn't have a main girl to spend time with or, better yet, go on weekend trips together. I decided I didn't want to be a player anymore.

This was my first year in the center. I was starting to gain status and become a leader. Every Wednesday in Job Corps, new students arrived usually around 7:00 p.m. The leaders in the center would gain access to the list. One day in particular, this cute little lady from Virginia caught my eye. She was five-foot two-inches tall and wore this cute little skirt. She wore glasses and was country. I saw her when she came into the center. My eyes were on her like Kevin Durant and basketball.

I told my boys, "She is going to be my girl." I took my time. I didn't want to seem desperate. The word was out around the center that it was hands off Cindy. I made sure no one claimed her. If anyone tried, there would be consequences. She became friends with Tony's girl. Tony was from Philly. He was about his business. I only hung out with brothers who were about hard work, education, and having fun.

Most of the brothers on third floor were about taking care of business. We formed a family. It was Tim, Tony, James, House, James, Eric, Jose, and Louis. Louis and Jose were the only Spanish brothers in the center. James, Jose, and Louis were on the second floor, but it was all good. We had Charleston on lock. I was going to get Cindy. She was lucky. I was the Muhammad Ali with the ladies. I was smooth, cool, and funny. I floated like a butterfly and stung like a bee. I was determined to make Cindy my honey.

I finally hooked up with Cindy. We became the Jay-Z and Beyoncé of the center. She was no longer Cindy. She was Flip's girl. She had access to all the privileges associated with being my girl. I was the happiest man in the center. I shared my uttermost secrets with Cindy. She truly became my honey. We were both from Virginia. We lived about a half hour from each other back in the state. She was everything to me.

The first time we were intimate, I was done. I felt like I was hit by Floyd Mayweather. We did everything together. You couldn't tell me anything. It had been a year, and everyone knew if you saw Cindy, you saw us hand in hand. Cindy had the whip appeal, and she whipped it on me. I didn't mind telling the truth. The truth will make you free. I was free indeed with a smile. We would take walks down the Kanawha River together during the evening. We would hold hands and sit on the steps. The water was beautiful. The air was nice. The evening was perfect.

You could walk down the river and, on each side, there were tunnels in the walls of the river. This was the spot for couples. You could walk down the river and see the birds and bees in action from either side. We never once went into the tunnel. We didn't use the tunnel. We were young, happy, and free. We created our own tunnel. Meanwhile, life went on every day. We went to the school infirmary and agreed to give permission to release our medical information to each other anytime.

The second year of the relationship became violent. She would hit me when she became angry. She did it in private. Eventually, Cindy decided it was okay to hit me in front of my friends. I put up with it from day to day. It was quite embarrassing to be struck in front of your friends. We were in line in the cafeteria and she hit me. She hit me so hard that everyone turned around. I raised my hand and hit her so hard she fell to the ground. She looked up at me in shock. I went back to my room and cried. I felt like I let my mother down. Her words were in my ear, heart, and soul. Whatever you do "never treat a women like your father treated me." Cindy and I continued in our relationship. She never hit me again after the incident.

Our relationship continued, but it was never the same after the incident. Eventually, I decided we should go our separate ways. Cindy didn't want to end the relationship. She came up with every excuse possible for us to stay together. I wasn't going to take her back. The word was out throughout the center. I recall Cindy telling me she was pregnant.

Cindy said, "I was scared to say something because I didn't want you to think I was trying to get back with you."

I was excited. I started thinking about us being together again with our child. We started making all these plans. We talked about being parents. A couple of months passed, and I became sick one day. I went down to the infirmary. I saw the nurse.

She said, "How is Cindy doing?"

I said, "Oh, you didn't know she is pregnant?"

The nurse looked at me strange.

I said, "She is pregnant."

The nurse said, "Flip, she is not pregnant."

I was really in shock. She said let me get the paperwork. Cindy came down for a pregnancy test but it came back negative. Are you sure? Yes, here is the test. I'm confused, hurt, angry, mad, and going crazy. I didn't know what to do. This had gone on for two months. During this time period, Cindy was playing it up. She was having morning sickness, cramps, etc. Eventually, it was time to expose the lie. I was tired of living a lie.

I shared with Cindy, "I know you're not pregnant."

She tried to play it off like I was joking. I reminded her that had given permission to release our medical information to each other. She was in shock. I got up and walked away. I felt like smacking her for leading me on for so long. I couldn't explain my feelings. I still loved her, but I was angry, hurt, mad, and confused. I thought about my mother and understood how you could still love and care for someone even after they hurt you. Eventually, we broke up for good.

It was rough the first couple of months. I had to see her every day and missed our time together. I was empty inside. My attitude about women changed after that incident. I went back to being a player. I didn't care about anything but getting mine. I was on a mission. I was out to search and destroy, but I was empty inside. I would date and be with all kinds of women, but I was empty inside. I didn't know what to do in my spirit. My flesh was satisfied, but my spirit was empty.

I reflected back on my mother. I reflected on myself. I needed healing to overcome this battle. The stronghold was powerful. I was never the same person. I stopped eating. I stopped being Flip. I stopped living a life full of joy. I reached to the bottom of my heart for help. The answer to my emotional incarceration came when I searched from within. My mother's words flashed across my spirit: "Make something of yourself, and never treat women like your father treated me."

The intimacy was over, and my mother was still alive speaking to my spirit. My mother died, but her spirit still lived in me. I completed my time at Charles Job Corps. I decided I wanted to attend college. Job Corps was going to pay for my degree. I attended West Virginia State University in Institute, West Virginia. I graduated from West Virginia State University and transferred to Virginia State University. My journey to Virginia State University took me back to my childhood. I remember growing up, and I became fascinated with magazines of naked women. They were all over my house. I would spend hours and days sneaking around with magazines. The seed of seduction was planted in my spirit. I knew I had the gift of gab. I was likable, smooth, funny, cool, and people were attracted to me. My experience in Charleston Job Corps took me from intimacy to seduction. I was over the incident spiritually, but my flesh was a powerful obstacle. It was a constant battle between emotions, flesh, seduction, and intimacy.

During my tenure at Virginia State University, I pledged Phi Beta Sigma Fraternity Incorporated. I wanted to be like my family members. I started seeking guidance and direction. I was seeking male role models. There was one in particular who really guided me without his knowledge. It was my cousin Benjamin Brown Jr. He attended Elizabeth

City State College, played basketball, and pledged Alpha Phi Omega. He would come home from college and tell me all kinds of stories. There was also Roland Holloway, who attended Virginia Union University and pledged Kappa Alpha Psi. I became motivated to be just like them.

They became the fathers I yearned for growing up. I loved being in college. My family and friends were happy. My father was proud. My sister had already completed her bachelor's degree. I wanted more for myself. I wanted my mother to be proud. I was on a mission to succeed. I graduated and worked for a couple of years. I decided to pursue my master's degree. I left my job. I moved out of my apartment. I applied to become a graduate assistant. I would have to live on campus and monitor the dorms. My first year was cool. You weren't sneaking any girls to the room on my watch. My first year of school was an adjustment. I had to adjust to living with freshman and giving up my privacy.

My second year was quite different. I was very popular on the yard. I was in a fraternity. I was in charge of a freshman hall. I was doing me. I remember sitting in the office on duty. How could I make some money? I knew freshman loved to party. I knew women loved to party. I knew the boys would follow the girls. There was one crew on the yard throwing parties. They were called New Jersey's Most Wanted. How could one person challenge the Most Wanted? What was I going to do? What kind of party was I going to throw? It took me months to execute my first party. For months, I plotted, planned, and executed my first party. The party was off the hook. I snuck up on the Most Wanted. I hit them with a left hook.

Everyone on the yard was talking about the party. My whole dorm heard about the party. I walked into the cafeteria, and people pointed and stared. "Flip, are you going to sit at my table?" I sat with my crew. My boys were stars! If you're reading this chapter, you're probably asking yourself, "What kind of party?" All the parties were at the Spotlight Café on Washington Street. Well, after attending several fraternity parties and watching how the girls responded to some of my fraternity brothers, the idea hit me. I'm going to requisition 10 guys to dance for girls. I'm going to pay them $100 dollars plus tips for 45 minutes. I'm going to rent the club and have my former students and freshmen promote.

I called my crew America's Most Wanted. I printed flyers, and the word spread like wildfire. I knew if the young ladies were coming, the young men would follow. My first party, 300 people showed up. I rented the club for four hours. The first two hours were for the ladies. I called this "The Show." The after-party was for the guys. This was called "The After-Party." The price went up. It was a Fiesta.

I wanted the guys there early. I wanted the guys there early so they could hear the girls scream. The line was long, and it was working to perfection. My security was in place. My crew was in place. The DJ was in place. It flowed like water. We didn't have to worry about alcohol. I had it all: money, women, clothes, and America's Most Wanted. I was throwing party after party. Eventually, two girls became part of America's Most Wanted. I only wanted them for a year. I called them Sugar and Spice. My conscious was killing me. I couldn't allow these women to degrade themselves for my personal gain. One of them had a son. I started thinking about my life growing up. Where is his father? Why is she out here dancing? Why am I validating this falsehood?

On the outside looking in, things were good. I was doing well in school. I had money, girls, and my crew, but it was all a lie. I spent days and nights questioning myself. The pain from my last relationship, the passing of my mother, the magazines, the abuse from my father, the seduction was complete. I needed validation from people who didn't know I cried at night. I needed validation from my customers. I needed validation from my friends. I needed validation from my crew. I needed validation for my flesh. I was headed toward spiritual suicide.

What happened next blew my mind. I saw this young lady. She was the epitome of class and maturity, and her spirit exemplified the love of God. She was everything a real man would take home. I pursued her to until she said yes! She became my angel.

She told me, "William, if you're going to date me, you can't throw those parties."

She was the only person I know who called me William. She was a keeper. She was different and down to earth. I had to make a choice:

Her or the parties. Well, time passed as we still were kicking it.

She said it again. "William, I mean it. "If you're going to date me, you can't throw those parties."

I had to make a choice. I will never forget throwing the last party. I remember putting it together. The same fire and desire wasn't there. It was over. My last party was complete. I went to see her the next day. I offered her money.

She said, "I don't want any of the dirty money."

I was shocked. She didn't care for the money. My emotions were crazy. I was so fascinated with this women. I introduced her to my family, friends, fraternity brothers, and my immediate circle. I very seldom introduced women to my family. I'm very selective and still am today. I'm a Virgo. She knew everything about me from my past to my present. I didn't hold back anything. I was honest and upfront. I was emotionally incarcerated, and she was my laxative.

Her spirit was so powerful. I wanted her to be happy because she relieved me of years of incarceration. I made sure all her needs were met and more. We were dating for about a year and a half. We were never intimate. It wasn't easy. We made love in each other's mind. She was my Eve, and I was her Adam. We would go shopping together. I remember one day, it was raining. I ran to the door because I didn't want her to get wet. We took pictures behind Puryear Hall. She was from the West Coast. She was in a special program and eventually would leave to go back home. I didn't want her to leave. I gave her this friendship ring. I spent some money on the ring. We spent our last night together. I remember holding her in my arms for the last time. For some reason, she missed her flight the next day. I wasn't happy my true friend was leaving.

One of the greatest joys in life occurs when you become emotionally vulnerable with someone you know who truly loves you. God allows certain people in your life to guide and direct you to manhood. We must be willing to search within the essence of our spirits and souls to free ourselves from our emotional incarceration. It's time for us as men to become vulnerable. You can't be a king until you're willing to look within and become vulnerable. This queen showed me what true men of God should exhibit.

What was your greatest takeaway?

_____

_____

_____

_____

What did you learn?

_____

_____

_____

_____

How does this chapter relate to you?

_____

_____

_____

_____

What will readers gain from this chapter?

_____

_____

_____

_____

What shocked you the most?

_____

_____

_____

_____

How did this chapter relate to you?

CHAPTER 7

The Inner Me Is the Enemy

"A man's spirit is free, but his pride binds him with chains of suffocation in a prison of his insecurities."

— Jeremy Aldana

One of the greatest challenges for mental health professionals is getting men to express their emotional secrets. It's a challenge that hinders men from reaching their full potential. It's like cancer in the body waiting for its time to kill. In some cases, those secrets cause death, pain, divorce, breakups, arguments, hatred, and frustration toward the people you love. I'm talking about those secrets you have locked away in a safe. I'm talking about those secrets that kill you emotionally at night. The one you wear to work every day — professionally dressed, portraying the illusion of success while, deep down, you're an emotional mess.

I'm sure there are some males out there who were raised in households where emotional release was normal. This is not the norm across America; we live in a culture where males prefer to keep their emotions to themselves. Boys are taught to be ashamed of the feelings they experience, so they grow into men who are emotionally confused and become victims of Emotional Psychological Incarceration. We teach our males that being emotional is a sign of weakness. However, from the mental health perspective, feeling more, expressing more, sensing more, experiencing more, understanding more, and releasing more is essential to the maturation process.

Emotions aren't meant to be suppressed; they are intended to be released. However, the longer you hold onto your emotional constipation, the more it leads to keeping secrets that directly or indirectly make you sick. The most powerful tool in my counseling toolbox is a mirror. The mirror is the gateway to your inner being. You will be surprised how hard it is for people, especially males, to look into a mirror.

In this chapter, I'm going to examine one celebrity and three men. Hopefully, their stories will resonate with your spirit and motivate you to release those secrets that are making you sick. He was once known as the "Baddest Man on the Planet." But despite the rage he exhibited inside – and sometimes outside of – the boxing ring, there was a little boy deep within who was crying out. This former heavyweight champion admitted in a recent interview that he was sexually molested as a youth. He told ESPN that, at the age of seven, he was grabbed by a man who attempted to pull him into a building. Tyson did not disclose further details of the assault.

"It made me have to be tough for the world I lived in,' he said. "It was no one's business to know. People just don't talk about it because, to some people, they believe it's emasculating them."

Despite "probably" feeling shame due to what happened to him, Tyson said he's grown to understand how it has affected his life. "I learned that it doesn't make you any less of a man because it happened," he said.

"Well I don't like to talk about that, I like to keep that where it was in the past, but I was molested as a child" (4). After reading that article, I thought about the thousands of young boys I've seen and counseled. I thought about the boys mislabeled for their behavior. I thought about the men I've counseled. I thought about the fathers of my students who sit in my office and release. This article was perfect timing for this book. It's time we put our ego aside and move into our destiny. We can't have healthy relationships with ourselves, others, or anyone at all until we look into the mirror.

One of the greatest entertainers of all time was Michael Jackson. He had a song on his *Bad* album titled "Man in the Mirror." This song is about making a change and realizing that it has to start with you. It was one of just two songs on the *Bad* album that Jackson didn't write. The song was written by Siedah Garrett and Glen Ballard. Let's examine the content. This song was deeper than just a man looking at himself in the mirror. It was the idea of a man going deeper inside to change from within.

We just examined two mainstream superstars who shared their secrets. What happens when the inner me is the enemy? What happens in public schools? I recall when I first started working with the Latin American culture. I didn't take the time to know the culture. I recall walking down the hallway. I kept seeing the girls hugging and sometimes getting very friendly with each other. I thought this was strange. I remember walking up on two young girls. I accused them of getting too close and kissing. They actually kissed each other on the cheek. I remember asking them were they going out with each other, and what would their parents think?

They gave me a look like I was crazy. "Mr. Clay, we don't go out. Why would you say that?"

"You don't think I saw you kissing? I caught you."

Finally, one of the girls said, "Mr. Clay, she is like a sister."

I was confused because we don't kiss our sisters. Well, I found out later on that their culture is very personable. It's normal to see best friends expressing their friendship for each other culturally. It took me several years to really understand the Latin American culture. I did learn one thing. They are family-oriented, and what happens in the home better stay in the home.

During this particular school year, I began to build a good rapport with my students. My students were beginning to believe in me as their professional school counselor. I remember sitting in my office. I saw this young girl walking toward my door. She was walking with her head down. You could see she was dealing with something. She sat down, and I began to observe her behavior in depth. I was quiet for five minutes. I kept working. We finally started talking. I didn't ask her directly what was bothering her because she finally was calmer but shook. So finally, after talking for about 15 minutes, I saw my chance to get her to share. She was ready. She was looking up. She was showing a sign that it was going to be okay. So I went into counseling mode.

I started asking more about her family. I noticed that, the more I talked about her family, the more her behavior would regress. I found her behavior to be quite alarming when we started talking about her family. She was born in the United States. Her mother gave birth to a son before she married. The brother was older than her and grew up in a Latin American country. They paid $6,000 to get him to the states. The little girl's father got him a job with him. They drove 45 minutes to work every day. The father and stepson worked together.

I remember the look on her face when I asked her for the name of her stepbrother. Her whole expression went flat. She was angry, shaking, hurt, and confused. I finally knew I had hit the jackpot. It was her stepbrother. I was very cautious from that point onward. I remember asking her how she felt about her stepbrother. She was quiet.

"How many people know what you're about to share?"

She stated only two people.

"How long have they known?"

She didn't respond. She finally stated, "This school year."

"What made you feel safe to share?"

"I was telling my best friend what's been happening, and she stated that I should share it with you because you would help."

She finally broke down and shared the secret that was making her sick. Her stepbrother would molest her when her parents were gone. This had been going on for several years. He was riding with her father every day to work. She broke down, and the secret was finally out. The years of pain released. The mother was contacted. She came up to the school. The father was contacted. He was on the phone, crying and upset. He all of a sudden got quiet. The father wanted to know if she was alright. She was still in my office. The mother was crying, wanting to know why she hadn't said anything? She was scared and didn't want to hurt him.

The father arrived at school. He grabbed his daughter and apologized. He was blaming himself. He felt like it was his fault. The student returned to school a couple of days later. She came by my office and said thank you. It was another day in the life of a professional school counselor, making a difference in the life of a child changed for the best. This particular day, I became a change agent. She was set free. Her life was spared.

You can't allow secrets to make you sick. The worst feeling in the world is living while dying inside. I recall my first year entering into middle school and counseling males. I was scared and ready! I didn't know what to expect. The boys were larger and older. They could speak, talk, and express themselves. I was ready for the challenge. My first goal was to start working with the young boys in the school. My first year was quite interesting. They were dealing with years of emotional constipation. My counseling was going to another level. I had to adjust and govern myself accordingly. I was blown away once the young boys started opening up and sharing their pain. It was like water flowing down a river. The more they released, the better they felt. It was so powerful that the boys would beg to make up weeks. I recall my vice principal attending one of our sessions. He started crying thinking about his childhood. Our boys saw us vulnerable. Our boys saw our pain.

They were so excited about our group. It was a safe place. I'll never forget this particular session. We were sitting in a circle. This was our fourth week. The first three weeks, we'd spent sharing our stories. They felt safe and not ashamed to share their personal details. I recall this one particular session. We were going around the circle. It was Jeff's turn to speak. Jeff was one of the most outgoing members of the group. He was the class clown and always spoke his mind.

Jeff said to the group, "I want to share something with you guys. I've never shared this with no one." He said, "Somedays, I feel like killing my father."

The room was silent. We just sat there, with everyone waiting on someone to ask why. Finally, one of the boys did.

Jeff said, "My father disowns me. He keeps saying I'm not his son. He treats me like I'm not his son. It hurts, but I don't like talking about it. I've tried everything to please him, but he continues to say I'm not his son. I asked my mother and she said, 'Yes, he is your father.'"

Jeff continued to open up more as the weeks proceeded. He would share his good and bad weeks with the group. Every week, the group was excited to hear good news. Jeff would share everything. It was a great relief for Jeff. I would see Jeff in the hallway.

"Mr. Clay, we are meeting today, right?"

"Yes!"

"Cool, I can't wait!"

Jeff was cool and smooth but knew his place in the group. He was the bodyguard of the group. He wanted to make sure boys were emotionally safe to release. Jeff's homelife wasn't stable, but he managed to help others succeed. I remember when Jeff left for high school. He would remind us of everything he learned in group. I was happy Jeff shared his secret!

The last 10 years of my career have been life-changing. I've learned so much about the Latin American culture. I've grown to love their food, religion and beliefs. I've grown to appreciate their culture. They are family-oriented. I've been blessed to help hundreds of girls overcome various forms of abuse, self-harm, and low self-esteem. In certain Latin American cultures, self-mutilation has become common behavior for girls. I recall days when young girls would bring their razors to my office.

"Dr. Clay, I don't want to cut myself no more. I'm afraid I will let you down."

Their friends would come to me and tell me who was cutting. "Dr. Clay, you need to speak to Cindy."

I felt honored that they trusted me. I recall this particular school year when Caty was on my caseload. Caty was sexually abused. Caty was an introvert. I will never forget my first four weeks with Caty. She wouldn't talk. She would walk into my office and ball up like a knot in the corner. She always kept her head down. I was determined to break through. It was hard; but on week five, she finally decided to open up! The first four weeks, I kept sharing my life story. I shared my ups and downs. I went deep into my personal life. She was listening. She was paying attention.

She finally allowed me to enter into her world of chaos, confusion, hurt, and pain. My first week of actually hearing her talk was beautiful. Caty began to share her timeline of events, which blew me away! Her life took a turn for the worst when she was three. I gathered from my experience that girls who are molested, raped, and suffer sexual abuse use art as therapy. They love drawing pictures to express their innermost feelings. I remember Caty drawing a picture with the words "lost," "ashamed," "suicidal," "depressed," and "alone" written out on it. I knew this was going to be tough. Her writings were powerful. I recall Caty writing:

I hurt people in a lot of ways, and they always cry after I end up doing something. I just don't know anymore because every time I'm trying to get better, there is someone trying to remind me of what I'm trying to escape from! Whenever people try to help me, I push them away, knowing the way I feel. I try to be strong, but it's just hard. I'm broken in every way possible. My life isn't as great as I could imagine.

I was raped at five. My parents separated when I was two. When I was seven, I had to choose between Mom and Dad. I choose my mom. My mom hits me for no reason. I have bruises. I'm the bad kid. I'm alone. I don't want to live anymore.

I knew my work was going to be crucial. My sessions with her became more interesting. I would find myself checking her stories to make sure she was being honest. I made some remarkable progress with Caty. She would share all the family secrets. She would share her personal, small secrets. I recall one day, I saw Caty at 8:45 a.m. and she was happy. Almost an hour later, she was in my office crying, having thoughts of suicide. She would talk about how she would kill herself.

I remember the mother coming to the school. The mother was upset because her daughter was sharing family secrets with a black man. The other counselor, who was Spanish, shared with me this knowledge. I remember Caty leaving, walking down the hallway. Her mother was talking to the other counselor.

I said, "Caty, your mother said we can't talk anymore."

Caty was shocked. She became upset. She was looking at her mother. I gave her a high-five, and she walked out the door. She was in school several days later. Caty came by my office.

"Dr. Clay, I'm sorry. My mother doesn't understand how much you have helped me. I still want you to help me. I'm doing better, but I do have my days. I'm not banging my head against the desk or wall, and skipping class anymore."

"Yes, Caty, you are doing so much better."

The following year, Caty was in the eighth grade. She would stop by my office and share with me her accomplishments. She was a new person. She wasn't perfect, but she was better. Caty began to see the enemy was the inner me. She changed her negative thoughts, conversations, and how she felt about other people. Her friends changed. She became the girl everyone went to for help. She was becoming the shining light for other girls stuck in darkness.

I remember speaking to a group of young men and their fathers. It took place in a small church. There were about 60 people in attendance. I'll never forget, after speaking and returning to my table, how this father and son walked up to me. The wife was a bit behind them walking up. I could see the boy was in tears. The father was barely keeping it together. The wife approached me and said thank you. I was confused.

"My husband has been dealing with some situations from childhood. He tries to hide, but he can't because it's impacting our son."

I approached the father. I pulled him to the side.

I said, "it's okay. You came for your son, but this is really about you."

He said, "Dr. Clay, you took me back to my childhood, and it didn't feel good."

"Brother, I understand. You heard my story, but it's time to release."

We did the manly pat on the back, and they left with a sense of hope, healing, and harmony.

What was your greatest takeaway?

_____
_____
_____
_____

What did you learn?

_____
_____
_____
_____

How does this chapter relate to you?

_____
_____
_____
_____

What did you gain from this chapter?

_____
_____
_____
_____

What shocked you the most?

_____
_____
_____
_____

How did this chapter relate to your family?

_____
_____
_____
_____

CHAPTER 8

Intergenerational Emotional Incarceration

"Sometimes we can't let go of the pain because we think it's the one thing holding us together."

– Terri Guillemets

The etymology of a word is its original meaning. In other words, it's a chronological account of the birth and development of a particular word or element of a word. Intergenerational Emotional Incarceration basically means negative behavior that is learned and passed down from generation to generation. It's the transmission of irrational emotional behavior triggered by trauma.

For example, when you go to the doctor for a sickness, the first question they ask you is: Is there a history of this disease in your family? Did your mother or father have this disease?

Irrational emotional behavior in males is often linked to the behavior of the generations before them. For example, the activity of their parents, grandparents, and family. Can we agree that parents are a child's primary source of learning? Furthermore, when parents display irrational behaviors, their children are likely to adopt similar kinds of behavior. Irrational emotional behavior can be the result of trauma, divorce, and adverse childhood experiences. Dr. Richard C. Francis' book titled *Epigenetics: How Environment Shapes Our Genes* concurs with how irrational emotional behavior can be traced back to learned or experienced behavior. Dr. Francis' primary basis is that stress in the environment can impact an individual's physiology so profoundly that those biological scars are inherited by the next several generations (*Epigenetics*).

For instance, a recent study showed that men who started smoking before puberty caused their sons to have significantly higher rates of obesity. And obesity is just the tip of the iceberg. Many researchers believe that epigenetics holds the key to understanding cancer, Alzheimer's, schizophrenia, autism, and diabetes. Dr. Francis received his Ph.D. in neurobiology and behavior from Stony Brook University and was a recipient of the National Research Science Award from the National Institute of Mental Health. I love the fact that his research validated how adverse child experiences impact us today.

What Are Adverse Childhood Experiences?

Adverse childhood experiences (ACEs) are stressful or traumatic events that occur in childhood. They may also include household dysfunction such as witnessing domestic violence or growing up with family members who have substance use disorders. For example, sexual abuse, emotional abuse, physical neglect, emotional neglect, seeing a mother being treated violently, substance misuse within the household, household mental illness, or incarcerated household members can all factor in. Once exposed to the trauma, the child tends to become stressed. The stress from the trauma impacts emotions.

In most cases, males are diagnosed with post-traumatic stress disorder. PTSD is described in the *Diagnostic and Statistical Manual of Mental Disorders*. The latest version of the DSM is the fifth edition. The DSM is the primary tool used by mental health clinicians. This manual is used to diagnose people with various mental disorders. This manual is as essential as the Bible to a pastor, the Quran to an Imam, and the Torah to the Jews. The essential feature of PTSD is the development of characteristic symptoms following exposure to an extreme traumatic stressor involving direct personal experience of an event that includes actual or threatened death or serious injury; or some other threat to one's physical integrity; or witnessing an event that involves death, injury, or a threat to the physical integrity of another person; or learning about unexpected or violent death, serious harm, or threat of death or injury experienced by a family member or other close associate. The person's response to the event must involve intense fear, helplessness, or horror. Or in children, the response must involve disorganized or agitated behavior, or emotional trauma.

One of the major challenges facing males, especially males of color, is feeling comfortable enough to seek mental health services. The evidence suggests that men are significantly less likely to use mental health services in response to a mental health crisis than women. This is especially so for black, Latino, and Asian men, who have much lower utilization rates than white men, as well as women. To break the chain of Intergenerational Emotional Incarceration (IEI), men must change their perception of mental health. We tend to believe mental health services are not finely attuned to men's needs, especially minority men's, which can be attributed to pride, perception, masculinity, stubbornness, and arrogance.

In my 15-year career, I've seen firsthand the impact of direct and indirect emotional trauma and how it's transmitted generationally if not treated. In other words, men who suffer from IEI are much more likely to suffer in silence, especially minority men. The men who suffer in silence become victims of substance abuse and, in some cases, commit suicide. Men make up over 75% of suicide victims in the United States, with one man killing himself every 20 minutes. Men living in small towns and rural areas have unusually high rates of suicide. Indeed, flyover states such as Wyoming, Montana, New Mexico and Utah have the highest rates of suicide in the country. Substance use is a predominantly male problem, occurring at a rate of 3 to 1 in comparison to females. Substance abuse is sometimes referred to as "slow-motion suicide" given that it can often end in premature death for the person concerned (10).

Another major issue men deal with is the "Mommy Syndrome." The Mommy Syndrome is the result of a mother who loved her son but raised her daughter. This often occurs mainly in the African-American community. A majority of males today were and are being raised by single mothers. Unfortunately, most men who grow in this environment have traits of emotional instability and respond very irrationally. The way they talk, think, and act is usually a reflection of their mothers.

This type of individual is being trained to think like a woman and act like a woman. He is spoiled. He lacks responsibility; he is ego-driven and sometimes arrogant. He beats his girlfriend over trivial issues and show high levels of possessiveness. He has a hard time with commitment. He wants a woman like his mother but never finds fulfillment. He can't take constructive dialogue because it threatens his imaginary manhood. He is a timebomb ready to blow because he was set up for failure. The men who suffer from Mommy Syndrome become easy targets for the system. They become so self-destructive and end up killing themselves slowly emotionally. They eventually end up in jail for committing crimes. Their behavior is a result of IEI.

The triggering of IEI in the African-American community is a result of trauma during slavery. For example, the father is murdered and destroyed in front of the mother, daughter, and son. The mother's natural response is to protect her children. Consequently, over time, she becomes more protective of the son. The daughter is allowed to mature. The daughter has now taken on the role of the father. She becomes the provider. She goes to college. She becomes the leader of the family. By the time black men enter adulthood, we are confused about our manhood. We are confused because we have been raised backwards. Meanwhile, our roles become confused and we become victims of the Mommy Syndrome.

IEI causes us to have insecurity. As a result, we never deal with the problem. We live in this fantasy world. We have children knowing we aren't properly raised to be men or become fathers. This behavior is passed down generation to generation. We see the results of IEI as a result of the trauma that triggers the syndrome. In closing, genetics loads the gun and environment pulls the trigger.

How do you overcome IEI? The first step is to not to deny it. "My mother did raise me this way."

The second step is to admit it. "I act this way because of my mother."

The third step is to understand it. "My mother acts this way because she was taught this behavior."

The fourth step is to appreciate it. "I appreciate that I know why I act the way I do."

The fifth step is to change it. "I must apologize and change. I must apologize to the people I hurt along the way."

The last step is implementation. The mother figure in question may be a grandmother, aunt, or family member. It varies according to who raised you! I was able to overcome my IEI because of my spiritual foundation. I was able to overcome because I refuse to become a victim. I was able to overcome because I didn't want to suffer in silence. I was able to overcome because of my mother. I was able to overcome because I wanted to overcome. There were times when I wanted to give up. I wanted to say, "to hell with everything." I would hear the words of my mother: "Make something of yourself and never treat women like your father treated me."

I would like to challenge the reader to write down or think about it:

I was able to overcome because _____!

I will overcome because _____!

I want you to repeat those words daily until it becomes part of your vocabulary. You must speak life and not death. You still can be successful as you struggle with IEI. If you're African-American, you will more than likely struggle with some degree of IEI. However, how you respond is essential. We go to work carrying the burden of IEI. We live our life carrying IEI. I will share with you major accomplishments in my life even though I was dealing with the impact of IEI and still do today.

It was October 2010. I would usually get up at six in the morning and listen to *The Steve Harvey Show* for inspiration. He would play a gospel song to get you going. On this particular day, he kept saying that anything was possible if you believe. He talked about the doors and his blessings. It stuck in my head like peanut butter and jelly. It was almost Hispanic Heritage Month. I wanted my Hispanic students to feel proud of their culture. What could I do? My school was 45% Hispanic-American.

We're a Title 1 school. My students' parents don't make much money. During this time period, the first Latin-American Supreme Court Justice was nominated by President Obama. She was all over the news. I walked into my principal's office. I wanted to make a rap video about the life of Supreme Court Justice Sonia Sotomayor. I wanted it for Hispanic Heritage Month. He looked at me a little strange. He eventually said to make it happen.

I selected 12 or 13 students. I called the group the Charles Carroll Tell' Em. I pulled the kids together. I explained the vision. Each student wrote a full-page paper on Sotomayor's life story. I put a song together. I met with the kids. We changed the lyrics based on their research. We practiced the song for several weeks. We shot the video in three days. I recall two of the girls getting into a major argument during the recording. I wanted to stop the recording. Luckily, the cameraman changed my attitude. We completed the project. I met with my students.

How can the justice say no if she sees this video? We invited her to visit the school. I mailed the video in October. The justice was now in office, and it was all over the news. Those kids worried me to death. "Mr. Clay, did you hear anything yet?" It was January. I was checking my email. I saw the words "United States Supreme Court" in my inbox. I forgot about the video. I read the email, and I couldn't believe it. I read it three times. I called my principal. I rubbed my eyes. She wanted to visit the school.

I came back to school the next day. I called the students down to my office. I remember showing them the email. I allowed one student to read the email. They were shocked. There is so much to this story. In April of 2010, my students and I met the first Hispanic Supreme Court

Justice of the United States. We were the first school she visited as a Supreme Court Justice. My students and I were featured in the *Washington Post* and performed live on Fox5 News twice years later. I thought about Steve Harvey. I thought about what was stated that particular day. It was his words of encouragement. I'm showing you the power of impact when you believe in yourself. Even though I was dealing with my own IEI, I was still able to find purpose in pain.

I want you to think about your purpose in life. What have you successfully done while dealing with your own IEI? For example, the welcomed birth of a child.

The second event occurred when I started the pursuit of my doctoral degree. I began in 2006, and my journey ended in 2011. During this process, my life went through so many changes as a result of my own IEI. There were days when I would reflect on my father: How IEI impacted him and how it was passed down to me. I would think about his comments. I remember after I completed my Master's Degree. He had stated, "I never thought you would become more than your sister academically." This was fuel for the fire. I wanted to achieve this goal to prove him wrong and make my mother proud. It wasn't easy going to school, working, helping clients, and running my business. I'm functioning but dealing with my battle with IEI. I was determined to make it. I wasn't going to give in regardless.

The journey of making it through this process alone can be life-changing. The mental whipping, hazing, and self-doubt placed on you can cause a mental breakdown. I recall failing one class and having to retake the class. I recall certain individuals blocking me from completing the process. I remember being accused of having an attitude and being an angry black man. My complexion was not my protection. I was angry because I knew my rights and I wasn't afraid to stand. I was serious about my success. I was determined not to allow certain people to hinder my completion. I had the evidence to show how I was blackballed because I took a stand. I had it in writing on school letterhead. I scheduled a meeting with the assistant to the president. I had copies of all my documentation.

The evidence verified what I knew. I was a threat. I was smart, intelligent, and black. I stood for my rights. I became a threat to the department chair. She didn't like it and put it in writing in so many words. During the meeting, I provided my evidence. The assistant was shocked. I was going public if things didn't change. I didn't want any problems. I was determined I wasn't going to become a victim of completing coursework yet not completing the dissertation process. The dislike was written. I was considered a threat because of my demeanor and melanin. I'm thinking about this situation and I said to myself, maybe she suffers from IEI. Did she allow her perception of black men to dictate her behavior? Was her behavior the result of past generations? I questioned myself: was my stance a direct impact of my own IEI? Did I deserve what occurred?

I marched across the stage in December of 2011. It was done! My five-year ordeal was done! I was Dr. William "Flip" Clay. I'm writing this chapter and paying attention to what occurred in Charlottesville, Virginia. We see first and how IEI can lead to anger, violence, and death. This type of behavior (thought process) was passed down from generation to generation. I will share the words of Reverend John Pavlovitz:

> Every white American needs to take urgent action to confront the scourge of racist hate. As a writer and pastor, my job is to weave together words so that those words will hopefully reach people in their deepest places; to frame the experience of this life in a way that is somehow compelling or creative or interesting, causing them to engage with the world differently than before. But there are times when to do this would actually be a disservice to reality, when any clever wordplay would only soften the jagged, sickening truth; when clever turns of phrase might succeed in obscuring the horrid ugliness in front of us. Sometimes we just need to say it without adornment or finessing. What we're watching unfold in Charlottesville, with hundreds of white people bearing torches and chanting about the

value of white lives and shouting slurs, is not a "far Right" protest. When you move that far right, past humanity, past decency, past goodness – you're something else.

It's necessary for us to say it – especially when the media won't, when our elected leaders won't, when our president won't. It's necessary to condemn it so that we do not become complicit in it.

The civil rights movement was intended to make Congress and Americans confront the fact that African-Americans were being killed with impunity for offenses like trying to vote, and enjoy the rights to life and equal protection under the law. The movement sought a cross-racial appeal, but at every step of the way used expressly racial terms to describe the death and destruction that was visited upon black people because they were black. As a result, one of the most interesting groups today is Black Lives Matter.

The decentralized Black Lives Matter movement burst onto the national scene following the 2014 police shooting of an unarmed black teenager, Michael Brown, in Ferguson, Missouri. As a result, activists have protested police brutality by stopping Black Friday sales, shutting down rail stations, and becoming a fixture in the eyes of black America. There have been several incidents pertaining to the death of unarmed black males. In Baltimore, the death of Freddie Gray in police custody caused concerns. After yet another high-profile death of an unarmed black man connected to police, there were riots, peaceful demonstrations, and proclamations from activists saying, "black lives matter."

Consequently, these demonstrations, have received plenty of criticism from aspects of American society. The majority of Americans haven't embraced the activists' message or strategies; fewer than a third of Americans said that Black Lives Matter focuses on real issues of racial discrimination, while 55% said the movement distracts from those issues, according to a September PBS News Hour/Marist poll. Another poll conducted that month by NBC News and *The Wall Street Journal* found that 32% of Americans had mostly positive views of the movement, 29% had mostly negative views, and 39% were neutral (11).

Does this country have a history of disapproving of civil rights protests and demonstrations? The movement of the 1960s speaks volumes. There are systemic illnesses, and structural defects, and national blind spots that we need to speak to and keep pushing back against. Intergenerational Emotional Incarceration is real across our country. The very nature of protest is fighting against the norm. Whether it is segregated lunch counters or voting rights, that's what protest does, and it challenges with varying degrees of intensity the status quo. Such behavior is considered controversial and violence promoting.

Black Lives Matter is a seed of the civil rights movement to a degree. The times seem different. The message is similar. The participants differ. In both examples, we see IEI in action. I want to challenge every male reader to answer the following questions.

How does it look in your family?

Are you suffering from IEI?

What caused yours to occur?

Are you in denial?

Are you ready to admit?

Are you ready to be set free?

How does this chapter relate to you?

_____

_____

_____

_____

How do you really think the writer felt?

_____

_____

_____

_____

What was your greatest takeaway?

_____

_____

_____

_____

What did you learn from this chapter?

_____

_____

_____

_____

Does this chapter relate to someone you know?

_____

_____

_____

_____

CHAPTER 9

The Excavation of Emotions

"One thing you can't hide is when you're crippled inside."

— John Lennon

Every day, millions of construction workers go to work. Those employees who specialize in excavation removal are called excavation contractors. In the world of construction, excavation contractors do much more than haul dirt around. Their responsibilities include site preparation, grading, trenching and many other soil-related tasks. What happens during site preparation? In a typical residential construction project, the excavation contractor shows up after the surveying crew determines the house and lot boundaries.

The contractor removes the soil to the depth required for the new foundation and ensures that the soil is firm through compaction tests and compaction with equipment, if necessary. The dig requirements are precise, so the excavation contractor must be able to use a level and transit to match the grade posted by the surveying crew. After the foundation contractor pours the footers and stem wall, the excavation contractor backfills around the new foundation.

Why am I sharing this process with you? The penalty for not following the emotional process can be steep. Let's get started. The objective of this chapter is to lay the foundation so you can excavate your emotions. The objective and goal is to develop a new emotional foundation

The word "emotion" can be frightening, shocking, painful, loving, peaceful, freeing, and much more. It describes life-changing experiences we manage throughout our lives. In essence, emotions are daily interactions within. If you really think about everything you do, emotions are vital in your daily decision-making. They seem simple, but emotions are complex. Your body and mind are together; therefore, emotions take on a different component. This is where things begin to get confusing.

It started out simple, but now we have complex beliefs, value-judgments, tradition, and morals. We use emotions to uncover those hidden beliefs and secrets. We use emotions to develop a better understanding of ourselves. We are taught who we are through life experiences, family dynamics, religion, and tradition, which in turn formulates our conditioning. Our conditioning can be an asset or liability. There is no such thing as a perfect person; we all self-reflect and internalize our self-identity, which become our self-judgments.

Your emotions are the best tool you have for exposing and coming to terms with life. There are five types of emotion: conceptions, sensations, reflexes, involuntary expressions, and voluntary expressions. Conceptions, sensations, reflexes, and involuntary expressions are biological adaptations. They are transmitted to the next generation through reproduction. They are universal to the humans. Voluntary expressions are cultural adaptations. They are transmitted to the next generation through interaction. They vary by culture. Conceptions direct your behavior. Conceptions are positive or negative mental effects that are triggered by conclusions.

Maternal love is a positive effect triggered by the conclusion that "my child is happy." Maternal grief is a negative effect triggered by the conclusion that "my child is dead." Conceptions do not trigger physical effects. Conceptions do not need to trigger physical effects to direct your behavior. A few conceptions do trigger involuntary expressions, which have a different purpose. The next emotion is sensation – for example, hunger, taste, and disgust. The next emotion is reflexes, such as fear. The next emotion is involuntary expressions, such as crying and blushing. The final emotion is voluntary, which may consist of anger and laughter.

Based on my professional experience, males can't manage their emotions. This leads to years and years of unfiltered anger. Anger is very toxic. It leads to pride and self-righteousness. "I'm right regardless; and if I'm wrong, you're lying." It places a shield against our other emotions. It causes males to blame everyone else for their pain. We hurt other people because it's too painful to look within. We become professional males masking emotions. It's time to begin the process of excavating our emotions. We begin healing by understanding history. The history of healing can be traced back to North-East Africa. The history of medicine, surgery, astronomy, and mathematics is also based upon the Egyptian Mystery System. Before we became programmed with Western forms of therapy (e.g., group therapy), our forefathers established healing circles. Traditional healing is not a religion, but rather a cosmology.

What are healing circles? In traditional African healing, the physical, psychological, spiritual, and ancestral worlds are interconnected; and traditional healers are the mediums through which these worlds are communicated. The first step is to establish a circle and develop a family-friendly atmosphere. The second step is building trust and confidentiality. The third step requires the introduction of the excavation process and how it relates to emotions. The fourth step is establishing ground rules. The final step is the pulling of the trigger. The trigger is pulled once I share my story. I use the term "trigger" because what's old has to die so you can be born again.

I started using healing circles in 2005. The results have been amazing. I've seen firsthand the power of healing circles. The ideal of having a safe place to reveal to heal is life changing. It's essential that every male find a place or group of men and start their own healing circle. A local church, mosque, or organization can do. You may start your own healing circle. One new paradigm in the field of counseling is called Man Cave

Conversations. The founder and creator is Mr. Todd Malloy. The whole concept behind Man Cave Conversations is to empower relationships, and share knowledge in the areas of sexual health, sexual intimacy, and topics beyond those.

The whole idea of creating the Man Cave Conversations is essential to the social and emotional development of men. I would love to see chapters of Man Cave Conversations throughout the world. Please google "Man Cave Conversations" for more information. I recall when I first got back into the church around the year 2000. The church had a men's Bible study. It was more of a Man Cave session. I saw brothers talking about infidelity, masturbation, pornography, adultery, and male issues in general. They talked about everything. I saw grown men crying and breaking down. It was intimidating because I didn't understand the power of revelation. I was new in the field of mental health.

Several years later, I found myself using the same techniques but adding my flavor. I called my meetings "Healing Circles." The goal of Healing Circles is to explain the importance of not disregarding feelings, the value of feelings, the release of feelings, addressing anger, self-reflection, and learning to love one's self and others again. I recommend males find a place once a week to disclose those tough emotional issues. My groups usually sat in a circle so that participants would feel at ease. The circle allowed the group member to build trust and visualize healing. Are you ready to start a Healing Circle group or Man Cave?

The second thing males must do is find an accountability partner. I'm not talking about your homeboy. If you're married, I'm talking about a happily married older male. If you're single, I'm talking about an older male who will challenge you mentally. If you're a young boy, select a male mentor. I'm not big on the term "mentors" because most men have commitment issues. I love the word "empowerment" because it validates the male ego. It's essential that every male have an accountability partner.

The third thing males must do is to use music. Music can be profoundly emotional and, in the last few decades, the use of music as a form of psychotherapy has become increasingly popular. I'm not talking about the music that typical Western therapists utilize. I'm talking about the drum. I'm talking about hip-hop. I'm talking about mainstream music that should be used more in therapy. Music therapy is multicultural. It's a very broad field, but the process can be helpful for a range of patients. I'm talking about 21st-century counseling, where counselors become more of the facilitator in music therapy versus the leader of the group. I've always used music in my Healing Circles.

Here is a prime example of how I use music in therapy. You can apply the process to your own emotional excavation. For example, I'm conducting a Man Cave Conversation group. My groups consist of males from 18 to 70 years of age. They are suffering from Emotional Psychological Incarceration. There are 15 men in the group. The first session is getting to know the clients. I'm explaining the physical excavation process and correlating it to the emotional excavation process. I've now determined their issues vary from anger management to divorce, relationships, alcohols, drugs, etc. The next two sessions consisted of establishing the foundation and digging (prepping the foundation). The third session is the start of the excavation of emotion process. My third session consists of grading and the leveling of emotions. I'm assessing to determine how deep I want to dig in the sessions moving forward. After the assessment, I determine what treatment modality, therapeutic theory, techniques, or strategies will be used to facilitate communication with the group.

The excavation of emotion process must be followed step by step. The facilitator may change the format based on the needs assessment. However, the goal is to stick with the process. The most important steps in the process are explaining the physical excavation process and how it compares to the emotional excavation process. Once this was established, we moved to the step of trenching. I'm determining how deep I want to go in each session based on the flow and format. The trenching process is important because, if done incorrectly, the participants will cave in emotionally. We aren't emotional by nature, so a sudden attack on our protective shields can be shocking to our emotions. This step requires planning, patience, and excellent listening skills.

The next step is using techniques that are traditional or non-traditional. I'm a non-traditional counselor. I use visuals, movement, and music. I would estimate 60% of male's emotional problems are the result of a father not being present in the lives of boys. The most challenging part of a healing circle is getting a male to talk about his father not being present. I've seen first- hand how men are constipated and incarcerated because they don't want to touch the topic. It's a little easier with boys, but it still can be a challenge. The great Fredrick Douglas stated, "It is easier to build strong children than to repair broken men."

Below is a sample session to use in a Man Cave Conversation. Our topic of discussion will be missing fathers. We have implemented the excavation of emotion steps. We're at the treatment stage. Let's set the stage. We have a group of men. I established the ages earlier. They are willing to meet, but the release is painful. They are fighting it, and you're stuck. What can you do? I go back to a universal language. I pull out auditory music. The primary goal is to get the conversation flowing without direct conversation. You want to facilitate, not counsel. The next step is to select a song that will guide and direct the flow of the session. The song must deal with the topic. The song must be age-appropriate and culturally appropriate. This will be determined during the assessment stage.

However, music is universal, so the selection must serve the purpose. I use two songs. I use "Dance With My Father" by Luther Van Dross and "Dear Mama" by Tupac. I share with the group that we are going to use music in the session today. We are sitting in a circle. I share with the group that we are going to discuss the song after it finishes playing. They are attentive. It's fascinating to see the response and anticipation...

What is he going to play?

What is he talking about?

What is going to happen?

The look on their faces is worth a million dollars. The look on the faces of males during the playing of the song is worth a million dollars. Let's examine the first half of the lyrics to the song "Dear Mama" as found on

LyricFind:

You are appreciated
When I was young me and my mama had beef
Seventeen years old kicked out on the streets
Though back at the time, I never thought I'd see her face
Ain't a woman alive that could take my mama's place
Suspended from school, and scared to go home, I was a fool
With the big boys, breaking all the rules
I shed tears with my baby sister
Over the years we was poorer than the other little kids
And even though we had different daddy's, the same drama
When things went wrong we'd blame mama
I reminisce on the stress I caused, it was hell
Hugging on my mama from a jail cell
And who'd think in elementary?
Hey! I see the penitentiary, one day
And running from the police, that's right
Mama catch me, put a whooping to my backside
And even as a crack fiend, mama
You always was a black queen, mama
I finally understand
For a woman it ain't easy trying to raise a man
You always was committed
A poor single mother on welfare, tell me how ya did it
There's no way I can pay you back
But the plan is to show you that I understand
You are appreciated

The first goal is to directly discuss Tupac's views on his life. The second goal is to discuss how the excavation of emotions is applicable to Tupac. The third goal is to discuss the excavation of emotion and how it's applicable to them. This will be guided by the facilitator. If the facilitator experienced the same situation, it is imperative he shares his experience to set the tone. The questions will be determined from the lyrics of the song. They vary according to the assessment and observation.

Below is a sample of the questions I've used in past sessions.

What is the name of the song?
What happened at the age of 17?
What happened at school?
Who did they blame?
What thoughts did Tupac have in elementary school?
His mother was a what?
What did Tupac finally understand?
Why was he angry at his father?
Who could he depend on?
Why did he hang around thugs?
Why did Tupac appreciate his mother?
How did Tupac feel about his mother?
How did you feel listening to this song?
How do you relate to this song?
Did Tupac's mother love him? Why?

The primary goal is to use the music to direct the flow of the conversation. I've seen firsthand how the mood of the room can change once the song is played and they begin to analyze themselves in reference to the song. The dialogue becomes easier, and the men feel safe. The process is in full force. Eventually, the concrete is laid. A new foundation is established, and the man is free. It's time for us as males to lay our pride aside.

Unfortunately, women outnumber men in therapy. Men tend to become ego-driven if they attend therapy, participating little, and dropping out. We tend to turn to alcohol, drugs, sex, and other unhealthy variables to fulfill our unresolved emotions. This is a very painful problem in the black community. We aren't used to sharing our emotions but, today, things will change.

It's time to release!
It's time be free!

It's time to let go!

Don't allow your ego to stop you from letting go. I didn't. What's your excuse?

What did you learn from this chapter?

_____

_____

_____

_____

What was your takeaway?

_____

_____

_____

_____

What stood out?

_____

_____

_____

_____

How did this chapter relate to you?

_____

_____

_____

_____

Did this chapter relate to someone?

_____

_____

_____

_____

How did this chapter relate to you?

_____

_____

_____

_____

CHAPTER 10

Traffic-Light Healing

"Healing doesn't mean the damage never existed. It means the damage no longer controls your life…"

— Akshay Dubey

I reached out to trauma-informed experts and educators around the country to get their recommendations for in-the-moment coping strategies and preventative measures to help everyday people process trauma. Mr. Donavan Dreyer, CEO of Get Ready Coaching, shared some valuable insights to helping young people with trauma. The rest of this chapter is his story:

I love a good challenge. My latest two challenges of counseling and coaching were initially selected in response to the shootings at Columbine. At the time of this tragedy, I was exploring which social service field to enter. For me, this event was a game changer in society. It became a mission for me to learn what makes teenagers tick and try to make a difference in their lives.

Right now, I am more inspired than I ever have been. Why? Because I have found tangible ways to empower parents and teenagers so that this world is seen as one full of opportunity that you feel equipped to make the most of and enjoy. It is my mission to get teens and parents ready to create greater success and happiness together.

I know it is a big job and that the world can be a scary place at times. I relish the opportunity to work with families. I will help you tune in to your unique challenges and guide you on the way to your success.

There is no substitute for an experienced professional with a solid foundation built from working with teens and their parents for 14 years. Below is what I call my secret sauce! Picture a traffic light. Do you see lights that are blue, pink, purple, orange, and set up diagonally? No. I don't care what state or city you live in, there is no place in the country where the lights are set up this way. Why do we have the standard green, yellow, and red? Some things are standardized for safety.

[The program] Solving Our Stress is designed like a traffic light with the same color scheme we already understand so well. I have worked with youth for 17 years as a high school counselor and life coach. I have learned that you have to see inside to prevent suicide. A common, universal way to look at stress levels is the key, just like we use the same colors for traffic lights in every state.

There are only three things you should do at an intersection. Slow down to stop when it is yellow, stop when it is already red, and go if it is green. Solving Our Stress is set up the same way. I teach kids, parents, and educators what to do when stress is red, yellow, or green.

I had a young man come in after getting into trouble. This wasn't typical for him, and I asked where he was on my SOS chart. He pointed to the upper yellow part. I need context, and SOS shows patterns by adding more to the "picture."

In the school, we don't go back in time and hear the whole childhood story. School isn't the place for therapy. The context for this young man came from simply asking where he was on the chart yesterday, the day before that, and the day before that. With this clear picture, I could see he was the worst on Day 1 of getting in trouble.

The problem the day he came into my office was obvious to see. His

stress level was on the verge of being worse than Day 1. His parents started doing some digging, and this made him worried again. Without any further details, you can see how powerful it is to literally see! A super-simple visual that creates a crystal-clear picture is worth a thousand emojis.

One step is to see the stress level. The second step is to take an action. There are only three internal conditions and three actions. Think about that for a minute. With all those different emojis to represent the variety of internal states, I say there are only three.

For the purpose of simplifying what to do, I have discovered that less is more. If you are in the green, you take action yourself, your coping skills help you deal with how you feel. If you are in the yellow, your trusted people in your life – family and friends, for example – help you deal with how you feel. If you are in the red, you need to go pro; you need professional help to deal with how you feel. This is the mental health emergency level.

To recap, the three types of help are: self, trusted teammates, and mental health professionals. If that red line has been crossed, you need to go to a pro. In the schools, we want kids to come to the counseling office. They can't help themselves at the red level. Their friends and family aren't turning the stress around. It is an emergency, so they need to seek mental health attention.

We seem to do this much easier when it comes to medical attention. When we are in an emergency situation with a medical matter, we go to the emergency room. Nobody in their right mind tries to "tough it out" like they might with emotions. If they do, someone is going to intervene.

We need to get better at intervening when mental health attention is needed. Now we have a simple, visual, common, universally understood language to achieve this purpose. Life is fun when you are prepared, confident, and capable. Get in touch today to find out more about how the services I offer can benefit you and your family. Text SOLVINGOURSTRESS to 33444 to get a free report with a more in-depth explanation and visuals.

CHAPTER 11

The Laxative

"People don't realize how a man's whole life can be changed by one book."

– Malcolm X

The emotional wellbeing of males goes through the stage of emotional constipation. During this phase of development, it's imperative that males start talking about issues relating to unfiltered emotions. It's during this phase when the signs of emotional constipation become evident. I discussed the symptoms in chapter 1. Human constipation, however, is marked by infrequent bowel movements or difficulty in passing stools. The correlation between constipation and emotional constipation is mindboggling. Both scenarios involve a degree of difficulty releasing variables. Constipation is treated by taking laxatives. They help with the passage of small amounts of hard, dry stools, usually fewer than three times a week. Before recommending the use of laxatives, differential diagnoses should be performed. In some cases, complaints of constipation may be

associated with other disorders. Consequently, emotional constipation causes males to act out accordingly. The ability of males to understand negative emotions requires the need for Man Cave Conversations, therapy, or a mental laxative.

Emotional constipation may not be a subject for polite conversation, but it's a condition that males suffer from daily. Emotional constipation is marked by an infrequent emotional   movement of pain. In essence, males suffer silently in pain. There is limited research on males and therapy. Therapy is perceived as weak, compromising every aspect of manhood. Men are taught to be tough, bold, and stand tall. We are taught to handle our own problems and that letting go of your emotions hinders your development. Unfortunately, there is a mask of falsehood many men wear. Underneath the mask, they are hurting because they haven't figured out a way to release their emotional constipation.

We live in an emotional illusion suffering in silence. Black men are particularly susceptible to this kind of unhealthy pressure and stress. The black male role requires us to be independent, tough, self-reliant, competitive, achievement-oriented, powerful, adventurous, and emotionally locked. The pressure from society takes a toll on males. As a consequence, males make it difficult for men to seek and utilize psychological services.

Men grow older into adulthood, with childhood dreams deferred because they don't want to release. Jay-Z articulated this in his song "Izzo" (aka, H.O.V.A.) when he said, "I've seen hoop dreams deflate like a true fiend's weight." The weight of the pain you decide to carry into manhood? Jay Z also stated that "you have to reveal to heal." One of the most popular songs out today is titled "Mask Off" by Future. In his quest for emotional freedom, he shares tales of drugs, sex, women, and cars. He repeats throughout the chorus the names of the painkiller "Percocet" and the recreational drug "Molly," aka ecstasy. The "Mask Off" title really describes the pain he is hiding behind because he won't take the "mask off."

Even in crises, most men will not seek therapy. We usually go based on the insistence of someone else – a wife, partner, friend, coworker, physician, clergy, or family member. Therapy can cause a great deal of

anxiety since most men don't like expressing their feelings. We believe exploring our sense of self can lead only to humiliation and rejection. This biased thinking makes it impossible for most males to find traditional therapy effective. In some cases, males will go to therapy; however, they come into therapy hesitant, reluctant, quiet, and resistant. Most of the time, they don't know or have little idea of what's wrong in their life. Historically, African-American males don't trust medical doctors.

We are less likely to see a doctor unless it's a life or death matter. We feel the same way about therapy. We don't want to share personal vulnerabilities. Most males, especially African-American men, see no need for therapy. We struggle daily with self-doubt, vulnerability, relationships, racism, sexism, and classism. It appears that men seek therapy only as a last resort: when their lives are in very serious trouble or absolutely chaotic. Seeing a therapist is in itself humiliating for men. "I'm admitting I can't do it by myself." This is counter-productive thinking that leads to shame, embarrassment, and what I call emotional egoism.

The therapeutic approach must respond to our needs, personally and culturally. The therapeutic environment is tilted against men, therefore we attend therapy with questions. We don't want to address feelings, words, emotions, and vulnerabilities and wounds. We deal with so many other issues daily and truly believe we can solve our own issues without seeking resolution.

The treatment session must address the impact of racism and the concerns of African-American men. Most African-Americans males, regardless of educational achievements and socioeconomic status, have, to some degree, been traumatized by racism. In addition, African heritage and cultural understanding will enhance the therapeutic relationship. Are you ready to remove the mask?

The older we get, the harder it will be to remove. The role of the male requires that men be independent, dominant, self-determined, competitive, goal-oriented, powerful, and emotionally restrained. These variables eventually take a toll on men's physical and mental health, and make it impossible for men to seek psychological services,

empowerment groups, or consulting. The traditional male role is that of "my way or no way. I don't need any help. I'm good." We become self-denying timebombs waiting to emotionally explode. However, once a man accepts therapy, it is imperative that the therapeutic approach employed responds to his needs, personality, professionally, and culturally.

Of course, the therapeutic environment has a negative view with men traditionally. Men come into therapy with a mix of questions, reluctance, resilience, and hope. They may be confused and have no idea of what's wrong in their life. In most cases, they've lost their jobs, drink too much, and have bad relationships, childhood bondage, and family problems. This is quite humiliating for men. "I'm admitting I can't do it by myself. I've become a walking corpse of shame, denial, pain, and anger."

You're probably asking how men, especially African-American men, get to this point of emotional bondage. My experience as a professional school counselor, speaker, and consultant leads me to understand that most traumatized behaviors start in childhood. This stage, I define as emotional constipation. I've seen the residual effects of emotional constipation exhibited in children, youth, and adults. In order to understand trauma in childhood, you must understand adverse childhood experiences (ACEs).

What are adverse childhood experiences? Adverse childhood experiences are stressful or traumatic events including abuse and neglect. They may also include household dysfunction, family problems, bullying, violence, punishment, whippings, lack of a father, substance abuse, etc. How and what society views as trauma is not the same for children and youth. ACEs are strongly related to the development and birth of health problems throughout a person's lifespan, including those associated with negative emotional behaviors. Here is a list of other issues given birth by ACE. They include physical abuse, sexual abuse, emotional abuse, physical neglect, emotional neglect, intimate partner violence, the mother being treated violently, a lack of a father, and substance misuse within the household.

There are several stages of ACE. They are as follows: adverse childhood experiences, social/emotional/cognitive impairment, adoption of health-risk behaviors, disease disability social problems, and death.

The Center for Disease Control has information about the ACE study, including the original ACE Study questionnaires and articles. In 2007, responding to popular demand for a condensed version of the original questionnaires, Dr. Anda created an ACE Score Calculator, which allows individuals to calculate their own ACE scores based on the original scoring criteria of the ACE study. To use this survey, add up all of your "Yes" responses. The sum is your ACE score. The ACE score can range from "0," meaning no exposure to 10, meaning exposure to all 10 categories. The study found that the higher the ACE score, the greater the risk of experiencing poor physical and mental health, and negative social consequences later in life.

Are you ready to release? Are you ready to ACE your reality? Are you ready to take the years of emotional bondage away? Let's began to start the healing.

Did a parent or other adult in the household often or very often... swear at you, insult you, put you down or humiliate you, or act in a way that made you afraid that you might be physically hurt?
If yes, enter 1 _____.

Did a parent or other adult in the household often or very often... push, grab, slap, or throw something at you; or ever hit you so hard that you had marks or were injured?
If yes, enter 1 _____.

Did an adult person at least five years older than you ever... touch or fondle you, or have you touch their body in a sexual way or attempt or actually have oral, anal, or vaginal intercourse with you?
If yes, enter 1 _____.

Did you often or very often feel that... No one in your family loved you or thought you were important or special; or your family didn't look out

for each other, feel close to each other, or support each other?
If yes, enter 1 _____.

Did you often or very often feel that... you didn't have enough to eat, had to wear dirty clothes, and had no one to protect you; or your parents were too drunk or high to take care of you or take you to the doctor if you needed it?
If yes, enter 1 _____.

Were your parents ever separated or divorced?
If yes, enter 1 _____.

Was your mother or stepmother... often or very often pushed, grabbed, slapped, or had something thrown at her; or sometimes, often, or very often kicked, bitten, hit with a fist, or hit with something hard; or ever repeatedly hit at least a few minutes or threatened with a gun or knife?
If yes, enter 1 _____.

Did you live with anyone who was a problem drinker or alcoholic, or who used street drugs?
If yes, enter 1 _____.

Was a household member depressed or mentally ill, or did a household member attempt suicide?
If yes, enter 1 _____.

Did a household member go to prison?
If yes, enter 1 _____.

So you've got your score. Now what?
I would advise you to visit the Center for Disease Control and determine how your score may impact you. Please remember that the ACE score isn't the final call; it's a roadmap. It doesn't directly take into account other variables. It's a roadmap to your healing. It's the first step

to release. It's your final release of years of emotional bondage. I would highly advise you to seek additional consultation. This may include group sessions, men's empowerment programs, counseling, coaching, or starting your own Man Cave Conversation group. The key is finding an environment where you feel comfortable releasing.

Once you release, your whole attitude will change. You will notice a difference in the lives of the people who mean the most to you: your wife, son(s), and daughter(s). The role of the father in the life of his children is priceless, especially in daughters. During my tenure as a professional school counselor, I can't keep count of the times I've been called father. It's a sad case when little girls don't have a farther present to guide, direct, nurture, and love them. They grow up seeking love in all the wrong places because their father was never present to guide, direct, nurture, and love them.

In most cases, girls act out. The mother gets mad. She is short-tempered because the baby-daddy is no good. She takes her anger out on the daughter. The daughter is upset because she doesn't see her daddy. This cycle is taking over America. On the average, over 55% of children are being raised by single parents. Our children deserve so much more from men. I'm challenging every man reading this book to shift. You must shift your thinking. You must say, "I'm sorry." You must become vulnerable to your children. You must go back and become the father you didn't have growing up. You must do whatever you need to do to get back in the lives of your children, especially your daughters.

Here is a list of what you need to do:

Be present, and not just physically. Your presence is mandatory. However, many times, we lose focus in the areas they need us most. Emotional, intellectual, and spiritual support is essential. Quality time is essential.

Provide safeguards for what they see. We are bombarded with negative images of girls and women daily. These images shape the way girls and women are perceived in society. These influences are on most channels. They are now on Disney, Nick, and regular television. What used to be good for kids isn't necessarily good for kids.

Be the type of man you would trust with her. What goes around comes around. The way you treat your daughter, her mother, and other women is what she will think is normal in relationships. I'm saying to release, and go get your daughter, and love her unconditionally.

Join a support groups for single fathers.

Confront your demons in the past.

Be transparent with yourself.

Be transparent with your children.

It's okay to say, "I'm sorry."

It's never too late to go back to your children.

Leap!

Who am I in this chapter?

_____

_____

_____

_____

What am I in this chapter?

_____

_____

_____

_____

When was I in this chapter?

_____

_____

_____

_____

Where was I in this chapter?

_____

_____

_____

_____

Why was I in this chapter?

_____

_____

_____

_____

What did I learn from this chapter?

_____

_____

_____

_____

How did this chapter relate to you?

_____

_____

_____

_____

Conclusion

The state of mental health for males is in a crisis. While the concept of mental health for males is nothing new, the heart of the problem is the ego. For centuries, the attitude toward mental health has been, "I'm good." Unfortunately, this is not the truth.

To be a male, especially an African-American male and mentally ill, is to face a particular challenge. Fortunately, strides have been made to put mental health and males in the same conversation. Understanding this barrier is only the first step to overcoming the many challenges in front of us.

Greater understanding of new and emerging mental illnesses for men is important. It's time for change. We must change the paradigm to start the conversation.

References

1. American Psychiatric Association. (2013). *Diagnostic and Statistical Manual of Mental Disorders* (5th ed.). Washington, DC: Author. Text citation: (American Psychiatric Association, 2013).

2. All Black & African American Communities and Mental Health. (2018, May 20).

3. Clay, W (2011). Post Traumatic School Disorder. n.p. Create Space. p. 11-12.

4. McAdoo, J.L. (1993). The roles of African American fathers: An ecological perspective Families in Society, 74(1), 28-35.

5. Hofferth, S.M. (2003). Race/ethic differences in father involvement in two Parent families Culture Context or Economy? Journal of Family Issues, 246-248.

6. All The Fatherless Generation (2018, May 20). Retrieved from https://thefatherlessgeneration.wordpress.com/statistics/.

7. Tamis-LeMonda, C.S., Rodriquez, V., Ahuja, P., Shannon, J.D., & Hannibal, B. (2002). Caregiver child affect, responsiveness and engagement scale (C-Cares). Unpublished Manuscript.
8. Killalea, Debra (2018, May 20). Mike Tyson on being sexually abused in childhood Retrieved from http://www.news.comau.

9. Etymology (n.d.). Retrieved http://www.etymonline.com.

10. Whitley, R (2017, February 6). Men's Mental Health: A Silent Crisis: Retrieved May 15, 2018, from https//psychologytoday.com.

11. Izadi, Elahe. (2016, April 19). Black Lives Matter and America's long History of resisting civil rights protesters. The Washington Post.

12. McAdoo, J.L. (1993).The roles of African American fathers: An ecological perspective Families in Society, 74(1), 28-35.

About the Author

Dr. William "Flip" Clay is a dynamic, innovative, energetic, internationally acclaimed professional school counselor and speaker. Dr. Clay has been featured twice on Presidents Day in the education section of the *Washington Post*. Dr. Clay has been featured on WTTG/WDCA Fox5 News in Washington, D.C., and on the *Steve Harvey Morning Show* (96.3 WHUR) with Mr. Tony Richards. After meeting Dr. Clay, the first Hispanic Supreme Court Justice of the United States, Justice Sonia Sotomayor, recognized Dr. Clay as an extraordinary role model and leader.

Dr. Clay is the author of *Post-Traumatic School Disorder*, subtitled *Empowerment Strategies for African-American Males.* Dr. Clay is the founder of Men of Ardmore (MOA), a data-driven, successful, elementary empowerment program. In 2011, Dr. Clay was recognized as the educator of the year by the Metropolitan Baltimore Association of Black School Educators. In 2012, The National Association of Black School Educators awarded Dr. Clay with the National Marcus Forster Distinguished Educator of the Year Award. Dr. Clay was the first professional school counselor to receive this award in its 20-year history.

In 2013, Dr. Clay contributed to the College Board Advocacy & Policy Center journal series *"Transforming the Educational Experience of Young Men of Color."* Dr. Clay is also a member of several professional organizations that include the National Alliance of Black School Educators, the Association of Supervision and Curriculum Development, American School Counselor Association, and Phi Beta Sigma Fraternity Inc.

A graduate of Charleston Job Corps, he holds an undergraduate degree from West Virginia State University and a graduate degree from Virginia State University. Dr. Clay is also a graduate of the American School of Professional Psychology at Argosy University in Washington D.C. Please visit Boysoffthehook.com for more information.

Made in the USA
Columbia, SC
20 May 2023

16404786R00075